Documents and Debates
Sixteenth—Century England

Documents and Debates
General Editor: John Wroughton M.A., F.R.Hist.S.

Sixteenth-Century England

Denys Cook

Head of History, Headlands School, Swindon

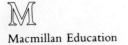

Macmillan Education

First published 1980

Published by
MACMILLAN EDUCATION LIMITED
Houndmills Basingstoke Hampshire RG21 2XS
and London
Associated companies in Delhi   Dublin
Hong Kong   Johannesburg   Lagos   Melbourne
New York   Singapore and Tokyo

Printed in Hong Kong

British Library Cataloguing in Publication Data
Cook, Denys
Sixteenth century England. – (Documents and debates).
1. Great Britain – History – Tudors, 1485–1603
2. Great Britain – History, House of York, 1461–1485
I. Title   II. Series
941.05   DA315

ISBN 0–333–24573–3

Contents

General Editor's Preface

This book forms part of a series entitled *Documents and Debates*, which is aimed primarily at the sixth form. Each volume covers approximately one century of either English or European history and consists of up to ten sections, each dealing with a major theme. In most cases a varied selection of documents will bring evidence to bear on the chosen theme, supplemented by a stimulating extract from a modern historian. A few 'Debate' sections, however, will centre on the most important controversies of each century. Here extracts from the changing opinions of modern research, normally found only in learned journals and expensive monographs, will be made available in manageable form. The series intends partly to provide experience for those pupils who are required to answer questions on documentary extracts at 'A' Level, and partly to provide pupils of all abilities with a digestible and interesting collection of source material, which will extend the normal textbook approach.

This book is designed essentially for the pupil's own personal use. The author's introduction will put the century as a whole into perspective, highlighting the central issues, main controversies, available source material and recent developments. Although it is clearly not our intention to replace the traditional textbook, each section will carry its own brief introduction, which will set the documents into context. The short, select bibliography is intended to encourage the pupil to follow up issues raised in the section by further reading – without being subjected to the off-putting experience of an exhaustive list. A wide variety of source material has been used in order to give the pupils the maximum amount of experience – letters, speeches, newspapers, memoirs, diaries, official papers, Acts of Parliament, Minute Books, accounts, local documents, family papers, etc. The questions vary in difficulty, but aim throughout to compel the pupil to think in depth by the use of unfamiliar material. Historical knowledge and understanding will be tested, as well as basic comprehension. Pupils will also be encouraged by the questions to assess the reliability of evidence, to recognise bias and emotional prejudice, to reconcile conflicting accounts and to extract the essential from the irrelevant. Some questions, marked with an asterisk, require knowledge outside the immediate extract and are intended for further research or discussion, based on the pupil's general knowledge of the period. Finally, we hope that students using this material will learn something of the nature of historical inquiry and the role of the historian.

John Wroughton

Acknowledgements

The author and publishers wish to thank the following who have kindly given permission for the use of copyright material:-

George Allen & Unwin (Publishers) Ltd for extracts from *Dissolution of the Monasteries* by Joyce Youings;

Edward Arnold Ltd for extracts from *Crown and Nobility 1450–1509* by J. R. Lander; *Reformation in England to the Accession of Elizabeth I* by Dickens and Carr; and *Government Policy of Protector Somerset* by M. L. Bush;

The Athlone Press for an extract from *Elizabethan Government and Society, Essays Presented to Sir J. E. Neale*, editor S. T. Bindoff;

B. T. Batsford Ltd for an extract from *The English Reformation* by A. G. Dickens;

Adam & Charles Black Publishers for extracts from *The Puritan Impulse* by M. M. Reese; The Bodley Head for extracts from *The Reformation in England* by P. Hughes; and *The Fugger News Letters* edited by Victor von Klarwill;

Burns & Oates Ltd for an extract from *Memoirs of Missionary Priests* by Richard Challoner; Cambridge University Press for extracts from *Cabot Voyages and British Discovery Under Henry VII* edited by J. A. Williamson; *Tudor Constitution* by G. R. Elton; and *Historical Studies of the English Parliament*; edited by Fryde & Miller;

J. M. Dent & Sons Ltd for extracts from *The First and Second Prayer Books of Edward VI* reproduced in *Everyman Library Series*;

Hutchinson Publishing Group Ltd for extracts from *Foedera XV* by Rymer and *Relations Politiques Des Pay-Bas et de L'Angleterre* reproduced in *Portraits and Documents: 16th Century* edited by J. S. Millward;

Longman Group Ltd for an extract from *English Historical Review*;

Oxford University Press for extracts from *The Crisis of Parliament* by Conrad Russell and *Select Statutes 1558–1625 and Other Constitutional Documents* edited by G. W. Prothero;

The John Rylands University Library of Manchester and Professor J. S. Roskell for an extract from his article Perspectives in English Parliamentary History published in *The Bulletin*, XLVI, 1964.

Cover Reproduced by courtesy of the Trustees, National Gallery, London.

Every effort has been made to trace all the copyright holders but if any have been inadvertently overlooked the publishers will be pleased to make the necessary arrangement at the first opportunity.

The Sixteenth Century

Until the early 1950s a seemingly unshakeable orthodoxy concerning the Tudor period had been built up by A. F. Pollard and other great historians. 'With the Lancastrian experiment of parliamentary rule, constitutional progress had outrun political morality. Law and order were first restored by the "New Monarchy" of Henry VII; his son's capture of the church then strengthened "Tudor despotism", and his grand-daughter harmonised absolute government with national sentiment; not until the accession of the tactless Stuarts, when strong government had done its work was this harmony broken and the conflict of crown and parliament began anew.'[1] The period presented the picture of a coherent age, increasingly 'modern' and separated from the Middle Ages by the twin phenomena of humanism and protestantism. Today little of this picture survives and debate rules everything. Recognition has grown that the date 1485 really means very little, and research, tackling questions of which previous generations had not even been aware, has dissolved former certainties.[2]

Changing views of the Tudor period have come about partly as the result of major developments in fifteenth-century studies in the last thirty years.[3] Until comparatively recently this century was one of the neglected waste lands of English history. It was still seen through the eyes of nineteenth-century traditions as 'a worn out helpless age that calls for pity without sympathy and yet balances weariness with something like regrets', as Bishop Stubbs put it.[4] The Yorkist age was particularly sterile ground: the Yorkists 'hardly knew whither they were going . . . (and) had little influence on the country for good or ill' (C. H. Williams).[5] Though well-intentioned the Yorkists had failed to deal with the problems of rampant disorder, aristocratic oppression and 'livery and maintenance'. Recovery only began in 1485, it was believed, with Henry VII who was the only fifteenth-century king to be acclaimed by historians.

Intensive research and the application of new techniques to hitherto unexplored and seemingly intractable sources has produced not only new attitudes to fifteenth-century problems, but a radical reinterpretation of fifteenth-century governmental structures, the bases of political and social power, the state of public order and of royal finances. All this work has created a deeper and more valid background against which the meagre, ill-informed, clumsy narratives of the sparse fifteenth-century chronicles can be more surely interpreted.

Similar and parallel intensive studies in earlier periods have also contributed to a reassessment of fifteenth-century conditions by providing more realistic standards of comparison than those which existed before. For instance the 'violence' for which the fifteenth century became a byword (largely because of the premature and isolated publication in the 1780s of part of the *Paston Letters*) can now be seen, from work on the thirteenth and fourteenth centuries, to be by no means an unusual phenomenon; whilst the publication of the letters of the Celys, the Stonors and the Plumptons has revealed that fifteenth-century conditions varied from county to county and from decade to decade. It is not now believed that violence declined very much in England until the last decades of Elizabeth's reign – this is an important point if misleading comparisons are being made between the 'violence' of the fifteenth century and the 'good order' of the sixteenth.

The researches of the last three decades have profoundly changed the traditional view of the fifteenth century in general, and in particular have led to a reassessment of the balance of achievements between the Yorkist and early Tudor monarchs. At a time when the fifteenth century to 1485 was virtually *terra nondum cognita* historians had laboured to define, for example, the main characteristics of the Tudor 'New Monarchy' producing a picture of solvency, efficiency, autocratic centralisation, the development of 'household' departments of government, such as the Chamber, at the expense of older 'public' institutions of government such as the Exchequer, and the use of middle-class men in place of feudal aristocrats. This over-concentration on the early Tudor period in particular, it is now recognised, produced a misleading picture attributing entirely to Henry VII vital reforms which it is now seen stemmed from his Yorkist predecessors. Henry VII the 'innovator' has now become Henry VII the 'adaptor'.[6]

At the same time as this reassessment of the fifteenth century has been going on there has come a reinterpretation of the sixteenth. For A. F. Pollard, the doyen of earlier Tudor historians, and others following in his footsteps, the main development in the sixteenth century was the establishment of 'national sovereignty', which freed men from the restrictions of the Middle Ages by establishing that 'order' which was the essential prerequisite of 'liberty'. The development was a gradual process: England was medieval in Henry VII's reign and not much had changed by 1529. Change really came with the Reformation and was completed with the Elizabethan settlement, after which the power of the crown declined. This evolutionary process was set out in detailed narratives rather than in precise analytical explanations of what happened.

Publications in the early 1950s (for example by S. T. Bindoff and J. D. Mackie)[7] marked the end of an era, for they provided the last chance to view the sixteenth century in this perspective. In 1953 appeared G. R. Elton's *Tudor Revolution in Government* which, together with his *England under the Tudors* (1955), *The Tudor Constitution* (1960), and numerous other volumes and articles in learned journals, has formed the basis of a completely new view of the sixteenth century. As he himself has written,[8] 'Elton has made an effort to see the century afresh believing as he does that the findings of research force a very different interpretative scheme upon the historian. He sees the years 1530–40 as the fulcrum of the whole story: in that decade, he claims, a still traditional system of government and ideas was so drastically transformed that the history of England thereafter, and only thereafter, developed along genuinely new lines. He emphasizes (no doubt too much so) the part played by Thomas Cromwell and treats the age of Elizabeth, in which the older tradition discovered the makings of a revolution, as essentially conservative. . . . All this work has succeeded in casting grave doubts upon the old concept of a "Tudor despotism".'

Elton's close attention to early Tudor administrative history in particular and his consequent view of Thomas Cromwell as 'the most remarkable revolutionary in English history', has proved to be the greatest bone of contention among historians. Elton interprets the recovery of the crown between 1471 and 1509 as the consequence of the restitution of efficient 'household' government, that is as a return to truly medieval methods. The real changes, he argues, came in the 1530s when the significant event was not so much the 'break with Rome' as the establishment of 'national sovereignty' – not in the Pollardian sense – but with the realisation that 'statute' was supreme, and that there was nothing that statute could not do, no field that it could not enter. This establishment of the 'modern' state survived the reigns of Edward VI and Mary Tudor to be consolidated in the conservative reign of Elizabeth I. Partly because of the collapse of royal authority between 1547 and 1558 the House of Commons was able greatly to increase its power after the death of Henry VIII, but even so opposition to the crown in the last decades of Tudor rule was less marked than in earlier periods; and the troubles of the following century were mainly due to the incompetence of the first two Stuart kings.

The very concept of a 'Tudor Revolution' where none was accepted before was bound to evoke protest. Elton's critics have pointed to the 'medieval' nature of the administrative machinery of government under Thomas Cromwell; and have argued that the bureaucratic methods of the 1540s – 1560s occurred at a time of weak royal authority. Recognisably 'modern' techniques of government, it is claimed, did not emerge until after the Civil War in the seventeenth century.[9] Partly in response to criticism but mostly as a result of his own researches, Elton has revised, modified and honed his views, but he is unrepentant. He can still write of his most recent work that 'The Tudor Revolution in government is still the foundation of the interpretation offered in this volume.'[10] It provides the underlying continuity between the 1530s and the 1560s and, for Elton, explains why the 'Mid-Tudor crisis' failed to destroy the unitary realm built on the legislative sovereignty of the king in parliament and the dominance of the laity over the church which had won the hearts of the political nation.

Changing perspectives, the discoveries of research, the application of new techniques borrowed from economists, sociologists, psychologists, statisticians and psephologists, the collaboration between historians and workers in other fields, have all contributed, and are contributing, to the rewriting of the history of the 'Sixteenth Century'.[11] The student who does not appreciate the reasons why every age rewrites history, or that 'History is what the historian says it is', who fails to see that the study and writing of history is a dynamic process, has failed to make an exciting discovery – or even to study 'History' at all.

On the other hand he, or she, can too readily assume that everything is in a state of flux and give up in despair; a balance needs to be struck between the 'old' and the 'new', the 'orthodox' interpretation and the 'revolutionary'. 'Historical study has necessarily become intensely specialised; its characteristic products are the monograph, the essay, the article, the 'note'. To make acquaintance with this scattered output is, of course, an essential part of the young historian's training. But in the process he may be so driven from one novelty to another, from the latest periodical to the latest *Festschrift* that he may become 'up-to-date' without being well-grounded, forgetting that the latest is not necesarily the last word . . . .'[12]

1   P. H. Williams, 'A Revolution in Tudor History?' *Past and Present*, 25 (1963) p 3
2   G. R. Elton, *Modern Historians on British History, 1485–1945* (1970) pp 26–7
3   The section which follows draws heavily upon the survey of fifteenth-century historiography contained in J. R. Lander's *Crown and Nobility, 1450–1509* (1976) chap. 1, 'Aspects of Fifteenth-Century Studies'
4   *The Constitutional History of England*, III (1878) p 613
5   *Cambridge Medieval History*, VIII (1936) chap. 12, 'England: The Yorkist Kings, 1461–1485', p 449
6   P. H. Williams, *Past and Present*, 25, p 3
7   S. T. Bindoff, *Tudor England* (1950); J. D. Mackie, *The Earlier Tudors* (1952)
8   G. R. Elton, *Modern Historians*, p 33
9   G. L. Harriss and P. H. Williams argued the case against a 'revolution' in Tudor history in *Past and Present*. See especially No. 25 (1963) pp 34–5, and 54–6
10 *Reform and Reformation, England 1509–1558* (1977)
11 For an historiographical survey of the sixteenth century see F. Smith Fussner, *Tudor History and the Historians* (1970)
12 J. G. Edwards, *William Stubbs* (Historical Association, 1952) p 20

I Aspects of the 'New Monarchy' c. 1461—1509

Introduction

Bishop Stubbs in his *Constitutional History of England* (1878), wrote of Edward IV that he was 'not perhaps quite so bad a man or so bad a King as his enemies have represented; but even those writers who have laboured hardest to rehabilitate him, have failed to discover any conspicuous merits . . . he was a man vicious far beyond anything that England had seen since the days of John, and far more cruel and bloodthirsty than any King she had ever known.' Stubbs, his own views coloured by his thesis of a Lancastrian constitutional experiment which had, apparently, been sacrificed by the Yorkists, was following in a tradition (first expressed in the eighteenth century), which went back to the fifteenth-century *Mémoires* of Phillipe de Commynes. He, anxious to show that Louis XI stood far above any other prince of his time, denigrated the latter's contemporaries, including Edward IV, who was made to appear debauched, cruel, avaricious, neglectful of his duties and indecisive in times of crisis.

John Richard Green was the first modern historian to suggest that Edward IV was not a 'bad King'. In 1876, in his *Short History of the English People*, he had given the title 'The New Monarchy' to the period 1471—1509. In his fuller *History of the English People* (published in the same year as Stubbs' great work), book V is devoted to 'The Monarchy 1461—1540'; and here Green suggests that Edward IV was 'a King of iron will and great fixity of purpose'. Green proved to be a voice crying in the wilderness. Later historians, succeeding to the mantle of Bishop Stubbs and following well-trodden paths in their interpretation of Edward IV, though accepting, and even closely defining, the attributes of the 'New Monarchy', shifted the emphasis from 1471 (or 1461) as the date at which the 'New Monarchy' began, and made Henry VII its creator.

The familiar scenario now ran as follows: the Yorkists had failed to deal successfully with the manifold problems which had confronted them. Not until 1485 — 'that almost mesmeric climacteric year' as J. R. Lander calls it — did recovery begin with the quiet constructive work of Henry VII. His careful parsimony established the financial recovery of the monarchy, and by pressure on the 'overmighty subject' through the court of Star Chamber he suppressed 'bastard feudalism' with its attendant evils of 'livery and maintenance'. He restored public order, cowed parliament and took the middle class into partnership against the old nobility which had, in any case, to a large extent destroyed itself in the Wars of the Roses.

Painstaking research over the last generation into hitherto unexplored fifteenth century sources – governmental records of accounts, judicial proceedings, administrative and executive orders – has shattered this picture at virtually every point. (Financial reforms, for example, which had been attributed entirely to Henry VII have been traced back to 1461; and no Tudor historian now holds the view that Henry VII suppressed all disorder through Star Chamber.) 'Such flights of imagination' (J. H. Hexter) have forever vanished – except in examination scripts which still contain the clichés embalmed by historians of the Tudor period eighty years ago – and with them the supposition that the date 1485, merely because of its change of dynasty, was in any way a fundamental dividing line in English history. 'The foundations of what has commonly been called the 'New Monarchy', wrote S. B. Chrimes in 1964, 'were laid not by Henry VII but by Edward IV.'

Further Reading

An essential introduction to this period is chapter 1, 'Aspects of Fifteenth-Century Studies', in J. R. Lander, *Crown and Nobility, 1450–1509* (1976), which has also been printed separately in a paperback edition as *Politics and Power in England, 1450–1509* (1976). The best general survey is by M. H. Keen, *England in the Later Middle Ages, 1290–1485* (1973). See also S. B. Chrimes, *Lancastrians, Yorkists and Henry VII* (1964), and his essay 'The Fifteenth Century' in *History* (1963) pp 27–40. *Fifteenth Century England, 1399–1509* (1972), edited by S. B. Chrimes, C. D. Ross and R. A. Griffiths, contains a number of essays including 'The reign of Edward IV' by C. D. Ross and 'The reign of Henry VII' by S. B. Chrimes, both of whom have also written full length biographies: C. D. Ross, *Edward IV* (1974); and S. B. Chrimes, *Henry VII* (1972). In *Crown and Nobility*, J. R. Lander reprints ten of his articles on the fifteenth century including 'Edward IV; the modern legend and a revision', which first appeared in *History* in 1956. Roger Lockyer's *Henry VII* (1968), contains useful essays and documentary material. Special topics are dealt with in B. P. Wolffe, *Yorkist and Early Tudor Government 1461–1509* (Historical Association, 1966); his *Crown Lands 1461–1536* (1970); and M. Levine, *Tudor Dynastic Problems 1460–1571* (1973).

1 The Evils of Misgovernment 1459

In this same time the realm of England was out of all good governance, as it had been many days before, for the King was simple and led by covetous counsel, and owed more than he was worth. His debts increased daily, but payment there was none; all the possessions and lordships that

5 pertained to the Crown the King had given away, some to lords and some
   to other simple persons, so that he had almost nought to live on. And such
   impositions as were put to the people, as taxes, tallages and quinzimes
   [*fifteenths*], all that came from them were spent in vain, for he held no
   household nor maintained no wars. For these misgovernances, and for
10 many other, the hearts of the people were turned away from them that
   had the land in governance, and their blessings were turned into cursing.
   The queen with such as were of her affinity ruled the realm as they liked,
   gathering riches innumerable. The officers of the realm, and especially the
   earl of Wiltshire, treasurer of England, for to enrich himself, peeled the
15 poor people and disinherited rightful heirs and did many wrongs. The
   queen was defamed and slandered, that he that was called Prince was not
   her son. . . . Wherefore she, dreading that he should not succeed his
   father in the crown of England, allied unto her all the knights and squires
   of Cheshire, for to have their benevolence, and held open household
20 among them . . . trusting through them to make her son King.
           An English Chronicle, ed. J. S. Davies, Camden Society, 1856, pp
           79–80

Questions

a Comment on the significance of the phrases (i) 'good governance'
   (line 1) (ii) 'affinity' (line 12)
b Identify 'the King' (line 2) the 'queen' (line 12) the 'Prince' (line 16)
   and the 'earl of Wiltshire' (line 14).
c What grievances against Lancastrian government are set out in this
   extract? What others ('and for many other', lines 9–10) have not been
   included?
d Explain the references to 'the knights and squires of Cheshire' (lines
   18–19) and she 'held open household among them' (lines 19–20).
* e What opposition was there to Lancastrian rule in 1459? How
      successful was it?
* f 'In the ten years since 1450 little or nothing had been done to remedy
      the manifold abuses of which the rebels under Jack Cade had
      complained. A list of grievances originally drawn up in 1450 could
      quite plausibly have been used again in 1460 to support the Yorkist
      cause.' Why and how in this period did opposition to Lancastrian
      misrule turn into a dynastic conflict?

2 1461: An Eventful Year

(a) . . . I also wrote how the people of London, the leaders of the people
of the island, together with some other lords, full of indignation, had
created a new King, Edward, son of the duke of York, known as my Lord
of March. From what we have heard since, he was chosen, so they say, on
all sides, as the new King by the princes and people of London. By the last

letters they say that his Lordship accepted the royal sceptre and staff and all the other ceremonies except the unction and the crown, which they have postponed until he has annihilated the other King and reduced the realm to a stable peace, and among other things, exacted the vengeance
10 due for the slaughter of his father and of so many Knights and lords, who have been slain of late.

> Prospero di Camulio, the Milanese Ambassador to France, 15 March 1461, in *Calendar of State Papers, Milan*, i, 58–9

(b) That day (Palm Sunday, 29 March 1461) there was a great conflict, which began with the rising of the sun and lasted until the tenth hour of the night . . . . Of the enemy who fled, great numbers were drowned in the river near the town of Tadcaster, eight miles from York, because they
5 themselves had broken the bridge to cut our passage that way, so that none could pass, and a great part of the rest who got away who gathered in the said town and city, were slain and so many dead bodies were seen as to cover an area six miles long by three broad and about four furlongs. In this battle eleven lords of the enemy fell . . . and what we hear from
10 persons worthy of confidence, some 28,000 persons perished on one side and the other . . . .

> George Neville, bishop of Exeter, to the papal legate Francesco Coppini, early April 1461, in *Calendar of State Papers, Milan*, i, 61–2

(c) . . . Firstly, if the King and queen of England . . . are not taken, it seems certain that in time fresh disturbances will arise. . . . If, however, they are taken, then that Kingdom may be considered settled and quiet under King Edward and the earl of Warwick; and then, as they are well
5 affected to the Dauphin [the future Louis XI] and the duke of Burgundy [Philip the Good] it seems likely . . . that they will pursue the plan to pass to France,[1] especially if the Dauphin did not happen to be in accord with the King of France . . . . I have observed the great importance that the duke of Burgundy attaches to England. . . . Two days ago letters arrived
10 here [*Brussels*] . . . and we have heard that it is true that King Henry, the queen, the Prince of Wales [their son], the duke of Somerset, Lord Roos [his step-brother], the duke of Exeter were taken, and of these Somerset and his brother were immediately beheaded . . . . Exeter escaped [*this fate*] because he is related to King Edward . . . . If it is confirmed then
15 before long grievances and recrimination will break out between King Edward and Warwick, [and] King Henry and the queen will be victorious . . . .

> Prospero di Camulio, 19 April 1461, in *Calendar of State Papers, Milan*, i, 69

20 1 An Anglo-Burgundian attack on France to divert French attention from Italy

Questions

* *a* What events had taken place immediately before those described in extract 2(a)?
  b Comment on the way in which Edward, earl of March, became king.
  c Which battle is referred to in extract 2(b)? In what circumstances was it fought? How typical was it of the battles of the Wars of the Roses?
  d 'I have observed the great importance that the duke of Burgundy attaches to England.' (2(c), lines 8−9). Comment on this statement.
* *e* How accurate was the information contained in the letters which arrived 'two days ago' (2(c), lines 9−14)?
* *f* Did 'grievances and recrimination' (2(c), line 15) break out between Edward IV and Warwick?

3 Foreign Policy, Justice and Finance 1475

. . . Consequently the lord King returned to England with honourable conditions of peace secured . . . . Some began to condemn the peace at once . . . . Others . . . took to pillage and robbery, so that no road in England was safe for merchants and pilgrims.

5   Thus the lord king was compelled to perambulate the country together with his judges, sparing no-one; even his own servants received no less than a hanging if they were detected in theft or murder. Such vigorous justice, universally carried out, put a stop to common acts of robbery for a long time to come . . . .

10   He dared not from now on demand subsidies from the English people in his necessity . . . [and] he bent all his thoughts towards gathering together a treasure worthy of his royal estate from his own substance and by his own industry. Summoning a parliament to this end he resumed almost all the royal patrimony, no matter to whom it had previously been

15   granted, and applied the whole of it in support of the charges on the Crown. He appointed surveyors of the customs in every port of the kingdom, the most prying of men, and, by all accounts, excessively hard on the merchants. The king himself procured merchants ships, loaded them with the finest wool, cloths, tin and other commodities of the

20   kingdom and, just like any man living by trade, exchanged merchandise for merchandise through his factors among the Italians and the Greeks. He would only part with the revenues of vacant prelacies, which according to Magna Carta cannot be sold, for sums which he had determined on, and on no other terms. He scrutinised the registers and the

25   rolls of Chancery and exacted heavy fines from those heirs whom he found to have intruded themselves without due process of law, as recompense for the issues which they had enjoyed in the meantime. These were his acquisitive devices, and other similar ones more numerous than can be conceived of by a man not skilled in such matters. In addition there

30   was the annual tribute of ten thousand pounds due from the French and

frequent ecclesiastical tenths from which prelates and clergy could not excuse themselves. Within a few years he had made himself into a most opulent prince so that none of his predecessors could have equalled him in collecting vessels of gold and silver, tapestries and precious ornaments for
35 his palaces and churches, in building castles, colleges and other fine places and in acquiring new lands and possessions.

Ingulph's Chronicle of the Abbey of Croyland, ed. H. T. Riley, Bohn, 1854, pp 474–6

Questions

* *a* What 'peace' was concluded in 1475? What were its main provisions? Why was it not universally popular?

   b Comment on (i) the reasons given by the chronicler for disorder in England (ii) his account of Edward's restoration of law and order (iii) his estimate of Edward's success.

   c 'He dared not . . . demand subsidies from the English people' (line 10). Why not?

   d Analyse and comment upon what the chronicler refers to (line 28) as Edward's 'acquisitive devices'..

* *e* 'Edward IV remains the only king in English history since 1066 in active possession of his throne who failed to secure the peaceful succession of his son.' Why was this the case if Edward was so successful in his own lifetime?

4 Papal Bull confirming Henry VII's Title and Marriage, March 1486

Our Holy Father the Pope, Innocent VIII, etc., by his proper motion, without procurement of our sovereign lord the king or of any other person, for conservation of the universal peace and eschewing of slanders as should gender the contrary to the same, understanding of the long and
5 grievous variances, dissensions, and debates that hath been in this realm of England between the house of . . . Lancaster . . . and the house of York . . . willing all such divisions in time following to put apart, by the counsel and consent of his College of Cardinals approveth, confirmeth, and stabiliseth the matrimony and conjunction made [18 January 1486]
10 between our sovereign lord King Henry VII of the house of Lancaster . . . and the noble princess Elizabeth of the house of York . . . with all the issue lawfully born between the same. And in likewise his Holiness confirmeth, stabiliseth, and approveth the right and title of the Crown of England of the said our sovereign lord King Henry VII and the heirs of his
15 body lawfully begotten to him and them pertaining as well by reason of his highest and undoubted title of successor as by the right of his most noble victory, and by election of the Lords spiritual and temporal and other nobles of this realm, and by the act, ordinance, and authority of

Parliament made by three estates of the land. Furthermore he approveth,
20 confirmeth and declareth that if it pleased God that the said
Elizabeth . . . should decease without issue between our sovereign lord
and heir of their bodies born that then such issue as between him and her
whom after that God shall join him to shall be had and born right
inheritors to the same crown and realm of England . . . .

>   Francis Hargrave, *The Hereditary Right of the Crown of England
>   Asserted*, 1713, pp xvi–xvii

Questions

a In what sense was Henry VII a Lancastrian (line 10)?

b Who was Elizabeth of York?

c On what grounds does Innocent VIII justify Henry VII's 'right and title
of the crown' (lines 11–12)?

d Why is it specifically stated that the succession to the crown *could* go to
Henry's issue by a subsequent wife? (See lines 19–24).

*   *e* 'The bull marks the beginning of the Tudor tradition of the marriage
of Henry VII and Elizabeth of York as the final peace settlement of
wholly dynastic wars.' Comment.

5 The Treaty of Étaples 1492

Meanwhile a peace was concluded by the commissioners, to continue for
both the Kings' lives, where there was no article of importance, being in
effect rather a bargain than a treaty. For all things remained as they were,
save that there should be paid to the King seven hundred forty-five
5 thousand ducats in present, for his charges in that journey, and five and
twenty thousand crowns yearly, for his charges sustained in the aid of the
Britons [Bretons]. . . . There was also assigned by the French king, unto
all the King's principal counsellors, great pensions, besides rich gifts for
the present. Which whether the King did permit, to save his own purse
10 from rewards, or to communicate the envy of a business, that was
displeasing to his people, was diversely interpreted. For certainly the
King had no great fancy to own this peace. . . . But the truth is, this peace
was welcome to both Kings. To Charles [VIII], for that it assured unto
him the possession of Brittany, and freed the enterprise of Naples. To
15 Henry, for that it filled his coffers; and that he foresaw at that time a storm
of inward troubles coming upon him, which presently after broke forth.
But it gave no less discontent to the nobility and principal persons of the
army, who had many of them sold or engaged their estates upon the
hopes of the war.

>   Francis Bacon, *The History of the Reign of King Henry the Seventh*,
>   1621, ed. J. R. Lumby, 1881, p 102

Questions

* *a* In what circumstances was the treaty of Étaples concluded?
  b What truth is there in Bacon's view that the Anglo-French agreement of 1492 was 'rather a bargain than a treaty' (line 3)?
* *c* Why was there opposition in England to this treaty?
* *d* What 'storm of inward troubles . . . presently after broke forth' (lines 15– 16)?
* *e* Why might it be argued that the main achievements of Henry VII's foreign policy culminated with the treaty of Étaples?

6 Threats to the Kingdom 1493

Trusty and well-beloved, we greet you well: And not forgetting the great malice that the Lady Margaret of Burgundy beareth continually against us — as she showed lately in sending hither of a feigned boy, surmising him to have been the son of the Duke of Clarence, and caused him to be
5 accompanied with the Earl of Lincoln, the Lord Lovell, and with great multitude of Irishmen and Germans whose end, blessed be God! was as ye know well: And forseeing how the perseverance of the same her malice, by the untrue contriving eftsoon of another feigned lad called Perkin Warbeck, born at Tournay in Picardy (which at first coming into Ireland
10 called himself the bastard son of King Richard; and after that the son of the said Duke of Clarence; and now the second son of our father [-in-law], King Edward iv, whom God assoil): Wherethrough she intendeth . . . the subversion of this our realm. . . . We therefore, and to the intent that we may always be prepared and in readiness . . . will and
15 desire you that, preparing on horseback, defensibly arrayed, four score persons whereof we desire you to make as many spears, with their custrells [attendant squires] and demi-lances [horsemen with light lances], well-horsed as ye can furnish, and the remainder to be archers and bills [men armed with halberds], ye be thoroughly appointed and ready
20 to come upon a day's warning for to do us service of war in this case.
And ye shall have for every . . . spear and his custrell twelvepence; a demi-lance ninepence; and an archer, or bill, on horseback, eightpence by the day, from the time of your coming out unto the time of your return to your home again . . . .
25 Given under our signet at our castle of Kenilworth, the twentieth day of July, 1493.
To our trusty and well-beloved knight and councillor, Sir Gilbert Talbot.

> Hatfield Archives, in *Letters of the Kings of England*, ed. J. O. Halliwell, 1846, Vol I, pp 172– 3

Questions

a Why did 'the Lady Margaret of Burgundy' (line 2) bear great malice against Henry VII?

b   Identify (i) the 'feigned boy' (line 3), (ii) the Earl of Lincoln (line 5),
    (iii) Lord Lovell (line 5).
* c What was the aim of the plot with which they were associated?
    What was their fate?
* d Why did the Perkin Warbeck plot prove to be more serious than the
    earlier one?
  e What light does this extract throw on the power of the crown at this
    time?

7   Extracts from the Private Account Book of Henry VII, 1497

January 7.   To a little mayden that daunceth, £12. To a Walshe man
that maketh rhymes, 6s. 8d . . . .
February 1.   Delivered to the Quenes grace for to pay her debts, which is
to be repayed, £2000 . . . .
5 February 17.   To the Quenes fideler in rewarde, £1. 6s. 8d. To the
gardener at Shene for graftes, £2 . . . .
March 17.   At Shene . . . Delivered and sent by the Kinges commandment to York, Durham, and Newcastel, £4000.
April 17.   At London – 21. At Grenewich . . . .
10 May 13.   Delivered and sent by the Kinges comandment to Berwik
towards the werrs, £6300 . . . .
May 24.   Delivered to the Coferer for 100 peces of Cornyshe tynne,
£250 . . . .
May 31.   Delivered to the Quenes grace for juels, £31. 10s. To a
15 woman for aqua vite, 5s.
June 5.   Delivered to th' embassadour of Naples, £66. 13s. 4d . . . .
June 9.   At Alesbury – 11. At Bucks – 12. At Banbury.
June 13.   At Wodestok – 14. At Abingdon. – 15. At Wallingford –
16. At Reding and Windsor. – 17. At Kingeston – 18. At Seint
20 Georgefeld – 19. At Blakeheth.
June 23.   At the Towre . . . To one that toke Lorde Audeley, £1 . . . .
June 30.   To two Ambassadours of France, £40 . . . .
July 1.   At Shene. Delivered and sent by the Kinges comandment
northward for the Kinges werrs, £12,000 . . . .
25 July 29.   At Netley – 30. At Wodestok. For sixteen pair of gloves, 5s.
4d . . . .
August 10.   To hym that founde the new Isle, £10.
August 19.   At Cornebury – 21. At Mynst Lovell – 22. At
Wodestok . . . .
30 August 30.   Delivered to Robert Courte for to be delivered to the
Kinges comissioners in the weste partyes, £333. 6s. 8d. To Jakes Haute
for the tenes playe, £10 . . . .
September 10.   Delivered to Richard Emson for to carry to Exeter for
the busyness ther, £666. 13s. 4d.

35 September 25.   To a man that come from Perkyn, £1.
    September 27.   At Cisiter – 28. At Malmesbury – 29. At Bathe – 30.
    At Wells.
    October 2.   At Glastonbury – 3. At Bridgewater – 4. At Tawnton. For
    the Kinges losse at cardes at Tawnton, £9.
40 October 5.   This day came Perkin Werbek – 6. At Tiverton – 7. At
    Excester . . . .
    November 3.   At Otery – 4. At Newnham – 10. At Bridport – 11. At
    Dorchester – 12. At Blanford – 13. At Salesbury – 14. At Andover –
    15. At Frefold – 18. At Basingstok – 19. At Esthamsted – 20. At
45 Windsor – 21. At Shene – 27. At Westminster . . . .
    December 3.   To my Lady the Kinge's moder's poete, £3. 6s. 8d . . . .
    December 18.   Delivered by the Kinges comandment in repayment of
    diverse lones, £3364. To blynde Cunningham, 13s. 4d. To the
    embassadour of Spain in rewarde, £66. 15s.
         Excerpta Historica, ed. S. Bentley, 1831, pp 85–133

Questions

a   What war was being fought in the north? How much did Henry
    spend on the war in 1497? How would this money have been raised?
    What were the consequences?
b   Explain the reference to Lord Audeley (23 June).
c   Comment on the item for 10 August. (See also extract 8.)
d   Why was a lot of money sent to the west country (30 August, 10
    September)?
e   Trace and explain the king's frequent changes of residence in 1497.
f   What do these extracts reveal about Henry VII?

8 John Cabot

Perhaps amid the numerous occupations of your Excellency, it may not
weary you to hear how his Majesty here has gained a part of Asia, without
a stroke of the sword. There is in this kingdom, a Venetian fellow, Master
John Cabot by name, of fine mind and a most expert mariner. Having
5 observed that the sovereigns first of Portugal and then of Spain had
occupied unknown islands, he decided to make a similar acquisition for
his Majesty.
   After obtaining patents . . . he committed himself to fortune in a little
ship, with eighteen persons. He started from Bristol, a port on the west of
10 this Kingdom, passed Ireland, which is still further west, and then bore
towards the north, in order to sail to the east, leaving the north on his
right hand after some days. After having wandered for some time he at
length arrived at the mainland, where he hoisted the royal standard, and
took possession for the King here; and after taking certain tokens he
15 returned . . . .

This Master John has the description of the world in a map, and also in a
solid sphere, which he has made and shows where he has been . . . .
Master John has his mind set upon even greater things, because he
proposes to keep along the coast from the place at which he touched,
20 more and more towards the east, until he reaches an island which he calls
Cipango, situated in the equinoctial region, where he believes that all the
spices of the world have their origin, as well as the jewels.
He says that on previous occasions he has been to Mecca, whither spices
are borne by caravans from distant countries. When he asked those who
25 brought them what was the place of origin of these spices, they answered
that they did not know, but that other caravans came with this
merchandise to their homes from distant countries, and these again said
that the goods had been brought to them from other remote regions. He
therefore reasons that these things come from places far away from them,
30 and so on from one to the other, always assuming that the earth is round;
it follows as a matter of course that the last of all mùst take them in the
north towards the west.
He tells all this in such a way, and makes everything so plain, that I also
feel compelled to believe him. What is much more, his Majesty who is
35 wise and not prodigal, also gives him some credence, because he is giving
him a fairly good provision since his return. . . . Before very long they
say that his Majesty will equip some ships, and in addition he will give
them all the malefactors, and they will go to that country to form a
colony. By means of this they hope to make London a more important
40 mart for spices than Alexandria . . . .

London, the 18th December, 1497

Raimondo de Raimondi de Socino, the Milanese ambassador, to
Francisco Sforza, duke of Milan, in *Calendar of State Papers,
Milan*, ii, 425–9

Questions

a Comment fully on the statement made at the end of the first
   paragraph (lines 4–7).
b What does the extract tell us about the career of John Cabot to 1497
   and his plans for the future?
c What light is thrown on ideas about the geography of the world held
   at this time by (i) professional navigators such as Cabot and (ii)
   educated laymen?
d What different areas have been suggested as 'the mainland' (line 13)
   where Cabot landed (June 1497)?
e Explain the reference to 'patents' (line 8). What else does the extract
   reveal about the relationship between Henry VII and Cabot?
* f What part was played by England in overseas exploration, discovery
   and settlement in the sixteenth century?

9 Renaissance England 1499

. . . But how do you like our England? you will say. Believe me, my Robert, when I answer that I never liked anything so much before. I find the climate both pleasant and wholesome; and I have met with so much kindness and so much learning – not hackneyed and trivial, but deep,
5   accurate, ancient Latin and Greek – that but for the curiosity of seeing it, I do not now care so much for Italy. When I hear my Colet I seem to be listening to Plato himself. In Grocyn, who does not marvel at such a perfect round of learning? What can be more acute, profound, and delicate than the judgement of Linacre? What has nature ever created
10 more gentle, more sweet, more happy than the genius of Thomas More? I need not go through the list. It is marvellous how general and abundant is the harvest of ancient learning in this country. . . . From London, in haste, this fifth day of December.

Desiderius Erasmus to Robert Fisher in Rome.
The Epistles of Erasmus, ed. F. M. Nichols, 1901, Vol I, pp 225–6

Questions

  a Who were Erasmus, Colet, Grocyn, Linacre, More and Fisher?
* *b* Why had the 'New Learning' ('humanism') taken a long time to appear in England?
* *c* 'Five men – William Grocyn, Thomas Linacre, John Colet, Sir Thomas More, and Erasmus, have long been regarded as the fathers of the revival of learning in England. In each of the five the new spirit manifested itself in a different way.' Illustrate and explain this statement.

10 Henry VII

Henry reigned twenty-three years and seven months. He lived fifty two years. By his wife Elizabeth he had eight children, four boys and the same number of girls. Three survived him, an only son Henry, prince of Wales, and two daughters, Margaret married to James King of Scotland,
5   and Mary betrothed to Charles, prince of Castile. . . . In government he was shrewd and far-seeing, so that none dared to get the better of him by deceit or sharp practice. He was gracious and kind . . . His hospitality was splendidly generous . . . But to those of his subjects who did not do him the honour due to him . . . he was hard and harsh. He knew well
10 how to maintain his royal dignity and everything belonging to his kingship, at all times and places. He was most successful in war, although by nature he preferred peace to war. Above all else he cherished justice: and consequently he punished with the utmost vigour, robberies, murders, and every other kind of crime. He was for this reason greatly
15 lamented by all his subjects. . . . But in his later days all these virtues were

obscured by avarice. . . . In a monarch it is . . . the worst form of all
vices, since it hurts everyone and distorts those qualities of trust, justice
and integrity with which a Kingdom should be governed.

> Polydore Vergil, *Anglica Historia*, ed. D. Hay, Camden Society
> LXXIV (1950) pp 142–6

Questions

a What evidence is there in this extract to indicate that it must have been
written between 1509 and 1514?

b What points (i) in favour of, and (ii) against Henry VII does Polydore
Vergil make?

c What *evidence* would you adduce either to support or to refute
Vergil's views?

d Compare this assessment of Henry VII with that of Edward IV. (See
extract 3). What, if anything, did they have in common?

* e 'It is always unwise to reject the verdicts of observant contemporaries
unless there are very strong reasons for doing so.' To what extent has
Vergil's assessment of Henry VII been modified by later generations
of historians?

11 Yorkist and Early Tudor Government Finance

Twenty five years ago, taking their cue from the researches of F. C.
Dietz[1] and A. P. Newton,[2] most writers maintained that Henry VII
restored the prosperity of the monarchy and based its organisation upon
the chamber. . . . [Now] B. P. Wolffe has published studies on the
5 crown lands which have so fundamentally changed our opinions on
Yorkist and early Tudor government finance.[3] In brief, the years
between 1461 and 1509 saw the rise, maturity, and in the opinion of
many contemporaries, the definite abuse of a new system of royal
financial exploitation, in the establishment of endowed monarchy with
10 the great bulk of the royal income coming from the customs revenues and
the crown lands.

According to Wolffe's thesis, from the Norman Conquest to the late
fourteenth century English Kings derived the bulk of their income from
taxation. . . . In the 1380s and after, the slogan, 'the king should live of
15 his own', became so popular as to be almost a political dogma, with the
house of commons and the taxpaying classes attempting to force the
principle upon the King, unsuccessfully under Henry IV, successfully
under Henry VI between 1450 and 1456. By the middle of the fifteenth
century the English landowning classes had become adamantly resistant
20 to any reformed, realistic assessment for direct taxation. Henry VI's
reputation had risen immensely when he agreed to conserve his own
resources by acts of resumption and therefore, to lighten taxation. Both
Edward IV and Henry VII grasped the significance of these dual demands.

Well aware of their insecure basis of power and wishing to avoid any
excuse for discontent, they were exceedingly circumspect in their
demand for direct taxation and raised in fact very little from it, Edward IV
no more than an average of £10,700 a year. Henry VII doing rather
better with £12– 13,000. Although both experimented with new forms
of direct taxation, their experiments turned out to be humiliatingly
unsuccessful.[4] Political exigencies therefore forced both Kings back on
the proceeds of indirect taxation (the customs system) the royal estates
and fiscal feudalism.

Edward IV in the 1470s imposed a new class of highly paid customs
supervisors in all the major ports . . . and Henry VII was constantly
preoccupied with the system. The customs revenues amounted to
£34,300 in 1478– 9 and rose to an average of £46,000 during the last
ten years of Henry VII's reign. Unfortunately, owing to the nature of the
evidence it is impossible to say what proportion of this increase was due to
improved trade and what proportion was due to improved administration.

A major, even greater thrust came with the royal lands. . . . In 1461 an
act of resumption was introduced to increase the value of the royal lands
and thus avoid the need for heavy taxation. Other such acts followed
in 1465, 1467 and 1473, and under Henry VII in 1485– 6, 1487 and
1495 . . . .

Equally important was a vital change in administrative methods.
Traditionally the exchequer had run the royal estates . . . [but] as early as
1461 the Yorkists adopted a new system based on the most up-to-date
methods of private estate management such as those of the duchy of
Lancaster and their own duchy of York . . . .

Henry VII, brought up abroad in complete ignorance of both
governmental and private administration, for the first two years of his
reign let the system lapse. Then, under the influence of ex-Yorkist
administrators, he gradually revived it . . . until by the middle of the
1490s Yorkist methods were more or less in full operation once more.

By Richard III's time cash income from the royal estates had reached
between £22,000 and £25,000 a year. (The land revenues declined to
about £11,700 in Henry's first year, most probably due to the exchequer
revival of the practice of assignment). By 1500 the estate revenues were
about two fifths greater, but the increase was due to further accretions of
land rather than to any further improvements upon the methods which
the Yorkists had introduced.

Edward IV's total income possibly reached between £90,000 and
£93,000 in his last year, that of Henry VII between £104,000 and
£113,000 towards the end of his reign. Edward IV was the first English
king since Henry II to die solvent. . . . Henry VII, so far from leaving the
fabulous treasures erroneously attributed to him by a Milanese ambassador (*Six millions of gold*) and afterwards exaggerated by Sir Francis
Bacon (at *£1,800,000*), left on the most reliable modern estimate no more
than a hoard of plate and jewels worth about £300,000, and certainly no

more than £10,000 in hard cash, or at the most no more than three years' income . . . .

In 1467 Edward IV personally announced . . . 'The cause why I have called and summoned this my present Parliament is, that I purpose to live
75 upon my own, and not to charge my subjects but in great and urgent causes, concerning more the weal of themselves, and also the defence of them, and of this my realm, rather than mine own pleasure. . . .'

But his subjects, and even more those of Henry VII, wished to have their cake and eat it. They not only grudged the King taxation, they
80 grudged him his 'own'. . . . Comparatively inefficient in all likelihood, as the royal revenue system was, it very quickly became all too efficient for their liking. Edward IV died with an unenviable reputation for greed. . . . On Henry VII's death Lord Mountjoy wrote to Erasmus that avarice was now dead . . . [and] Sir Thomas More felt it safe enough to
85 greet the new King with Latin poems denouncing his father's greed and the maleficent actions of his agents.

J. R. Lander, *Crown and Nobility 1450–1509*, 1976, pp 38–42

1 *English Government Finance, 1485–1558* (1920)
2 'The King's Chamber under the Early Tudors', *EHR* XXXII (1917) pp 348–72
3 *The Crown Lands, 1461–1536* (1970) pp 1–28
4 See S. B. Chrimes, *Henry VII* (1972) pp 198–201

Questions

a Why has there been a fundamental change in historians' views about Yorkist and early Tudor government finance?
b To what extent has this interpretation altered judgements about the financial achievements of Henry VII?
c What do you understand by the phrase 'the King should live of his own' (line 14–15)?
d What were the principal sources of royal revenue under Edward IV and Henry VII? How was this money administered?
e How would you explain the apparent paradox – that both Edward IV and Henry VII died with 'an unenviable reputation for greed' – when they both raised so little money by direct taxation?
* f Comment on the view that, by failing to raise more money by direct taxation, both Edward IV and Henry VII gravely weakened the power of the crown.

II Cardinal Wolsey

Introduction

'Few men of eminence and ability can ever have had a worse press than Thomas Wolsey, butcher's son and prince of the Church.'[1] Of his contemporaries only his gentleman-usher, George Cavendish, writing in the 1550s, had a good word to say for him. Wolsey was execrated by, among others, Polydore Vergil, John Skelton and Edward Hall. The picture they drew of the 'evil genius' of Henry VIII has come down into modern times through the pages of Shakespeare and the celluloid of Hollywood.

The really surprising fact about Wolsey, however, is that he has attracted so little attention from modern historians. In the last century only two books of any consequence have been devoted entirely to him: Bishop Creighton, *Cardinal Wolsey* (1888), and A. F. Pollard, *Wolsey* (1929). The former, written under the shadow of Bismarck, depicted Wolsey the patriot and concentrated exclusively on foreign policy. The latter did ample justice to Wolsey's domestic policy but, written by a man who 'admired, almost worshipped Henry VIII', was bound to lead to a corresponding depreciation of his minister.[2] This book 'the best book on Wolsey so far written', is, says G. R. Elton,[3] largely responsible for the present low estimation of Wolsey, whose record is usually seen as 'one of failure', and 'sterility' as the keynote of his fifteen year ascendancy.

'Not a great deal of work has been done on the age of Wolsey since Pollard wrote',[4] but there has been some. For example, Pollard's thesis, that Wolsey totally subordinated England's interests to those of the papacy in his conduct of foreign policy, and that he was motivated, primarily, by an over-riding desire to be pope, has been challenged.[5]

'Pollard's interpretation was seriously mistaken. Wolsey was much less free to do as he pleased than Pollard supposed, and the mainsprings of his action would seem to have been the dynastic interests of the crown, the King's personal desire for glory, and the cardinal's genuine desire to stand forth as a peace maker. The last ambition usually conflicted with the other two and usually came off worst.'[6]

As an administrator Wolsey has been promoted from 'moderately inspired amateur' (1965), to 'superb amateur in government' (1977).[7] This is the result of research into his temporal activities, most recently, and notably, into his work in Star Chamber.[8] This has caused one reviewer to exclaim, 'Now we are coming to understand *why* Wolsey ruled the country with success for so long.'[9]

This view of Wolsey 'the success' is in contrast to the more traditional verdict, which sees him as 'responsible for an often mistaken and ultimately disastrous foreign policy, amateurish and uncreative in the government of the realm, only moderately successful in ruling its Church. . . .'[10] This verdict is usually tempered only by the (grudging) assertion that Wolsey taught Henry VIII 'the way to control the Church and, by default, instructed him in the use of Parliament and nation';[11] or by the view that Wolsey's importance lies in what he did during his tenure of power, and that 'to call him nothing but a failure is to judge him by what happened after he ceased to be'.[12]

But new questions are being posed. Can Wolsey really be blamed for the failure of 'his'[13] foreign policy by 1529?[14] And was it so entirely wrong?[15] Were there no 'institutional' legacies?[16] Did he really do nothing but damage to the church, leaving it 'brow beaten and dispirited'?[17] (If so, why was there so much opposition from the church in the early 1530s?)

Could it be that as the 450th anniversary of his death approaches Thomas Wolsey is about to be established, if not as 'the greatest statesman England ever produced',[18] at least as 'by far the greatest chancellor England ever had'?[19] Certainly 'Wolsey must go up in historical estimation'.[20]

1   G. R. Elton, *Studies in Tudor and Stuart Politics and Government* (1974) I, p 109
2   Elton, *Studies*, I, p 111
3   *Studies*, I, p 114
4   *Studies*, I, p 115
5   See, for example, R. B. Wernham, *Before the Armada: the growth of English foreign policy 1485–1588* (1966); J. J. Scarisbrick, *Henry VIII* (1968); P. S. Crowson, *Tudor Foreign Policy* (1974); and extract 5 below
6   Elton, *England under the Tudors* (2nd ed. 1974) p 477
7   Compare Elton, *Studies*, I, p 120, with the same author's *Reform and Reformation* (1977) p 62
8   J. A. Guy, *The Cardinal's Court: the Impact of Thomas Wolsey in Star Chamber* (1977)
9   A. L. Rowse, *History Today*, March 1978, p 202
10 Elton, *Studies*, I, p 125
11 Elton, paraphrasing A. F. Pollard, *Studies*, I, p 127. For a contrary view see Scarisbrick, op. cit., p 316; Elton, *Studies*, I, p 127
12 Elton, *Studies*, I, p 126. See also C. S. L. Davies, *Peace, Print and Protestantism* (1976) p 176
13 On this point see, for example, Scarisbrick, op. cit., p 72. Compare with Elton, *Reform and Reformation*, p 85
14 See Davies, op. cit., p 176
15 See J. D. Mackie, *The Earlier Tudors 1485–1558* (1952) p 333
16 J. A. Guy, op. cit., writes 'Without the vision and originality of Thomas Wolsey . . . the Council in Star Chamber would not have realised its full potential.'
17 A. F. Pollard
18 E. L. Taunton, *Thomas Wolsey, Legate and Reformer* (1906) p 3
19 Quoted by Mackie, op. cit., p 295
20 A. L. Rowse, loc. cit.

Further Reading

An essential introduction is the essay by G. R. Elton first published in 1965 as the introduction to the Fontana edition of A. F. Pollard, *Wolsey*. It has been reprinted, with footnotes, in Elton, *Studies in Tudor and Stuart Politics and Government* (1974) I, pp 109–28. The most recent standard textbook accounts of Wolsey are C. S. L. Davies, *Peace, Print and Protestantism* (1976) pp 156–76, and G. R. Elton, *Reform and Reformation* (1977) pp 42–115. The most recent book on Wolsey is J. A. Guy, *The Cardinal's Court: the Impact of Thomas Wolsey in Star Chamber (1977)*. See also C. W. Ferguson, *Naked to Mine Enemies. The Life of Cardinal Wolsey* (1958, repr. 1973); Neville Williams, *The Cardinal and the Secretary* (1975). For the revolt of 1525 see Anthony Fletcher, *Tudor Rebellions* (1968) pp 17–20.

1 Wolsey — Cardinal Archbishop

. . . The King [Henry VII] . . . gave him . . . for his diligent and faithful service the Deanery of Lincoln, which . . . was one of the worthiest spiritual promotions that he gave under the degree of a bishopric . . . .

[He] handled himself so subtly that he found the means to be one of the
5 King's [Henry VIII's] council. . . . After the King's return [from France 1514] the see of Lincoln fell void . . . and this benefice and promotion His Grace gave unto his Almoner [1509], Bishop elect of Tournai. . . . It was not long afterwards that Doctor Bainbridge, Archbishop of York, died at Rome . . . Unto which benefice the King presented his new
10 Bishop of Lincoln, so that he had three bishoprics in one year given him . . . .

. . . He, being in possession of the Archbishopric of York . . . thought himself sufficient to compare with [the Archbishop of] Canterbury . . . [and] intended to provide some such means that he would
15 rather be superior in dignity to Canterbury than be either obedient or equal to him. Wherefore he contrived first to be made Priest Cardinal, and then later *legatus a latere* . . . .

Now he, being . . . endowed with the promotions of an Archbishop, and also Cardinal Legate *a latere*, thought himself fully furnished with
20 such authorities and dignities that he was able to surmount Canterbury in all ecclesiastical jurisdictions. He had power to convocate Canterbury, and other bishops within his province, to assemble at his convocation in any place within this realm where he would assign. He took upon him the correction of all matters in every diocese, having there through all the
25 realm all manner of spiritual ministers, such as commissaries, scribes, apparitors, and all other officers to furnish his courts. He visited also all spiritual houses, and presented . . . whom he liked to their benefices.

. . . And to the increase of his gains he had also the bishopric of Durham, and the Abbey of St. Albans *in commendam*. . . . When Bishop
30 Fox of Winchester died, he surrendered Durham and in lieu thereof took

Winchester. Then he held also . . . *in ferme* both [*sic*] Bath and Worcester and Hereford, because the incumbents thereof were strangers . . . remaining always beyond the seas in their own native countries . . . .

George Cavendish, *The Life and Death of Cardinal Wolsey*, ed. R. S. Sylvester, Early English Text Society, 1959

Questions

* a What is known about Wolsey's origins and early life?
  b What were the principal ecclesiastical appointments which were held by Wolsey directly?
  c How did Wolsey 'contrive . . . to be made Priest Cardinal' (line 16)?
  d Explain the meaning of (i) *legatus a latere* (line 17) (ii) *in commendam (line 29)* (iii) *in ferme* (line 31).
  e What ecclesiastical power was wielded by Wolsey?
* f 'In ecclesiastical affairs the story is one of missed opportunities. Wolsey talked a good deal of reform, and did nothing.' Comment.
* g Who was George Cavendish? How important is his account of Wolsey?

2 Wolsey — Lord Chancellor

Now will I declare unto you his order in going to Westminster Hall daily in the term season. First, before his coming out of his private chamber, he heard most commonly every day two masses in his private closet, and there said his daily service with his chaplain. . . . The Cardinal, what-
5 soever business or weighty matters he had in the day, never went to his bed with any part of his divine service unsaid, yea not so much as one collect; wherein I doubt not but he deceived the opinion of divers persons . . . .

He would issue out apparelled all in red,· in the habit of a
10 cardinal . . . the best that money could buy. And upon his head a round pillion, with a neck of black velvet . . . he also had a tippet of fine sables about his neck . . . .

There was also borne before him, first the great seal of England, and then his cardinal's hat, by a nobleman or some worthy gentleman, right
15 solemnly, bareheaded. . . . [In his presence Chamber] he found – attending his coming, to await upon him to Westminister Hall – as well noblemen and other worthy gentlemen and noblemen and gentlemen of his own household. Thus he passed forth, with two great crosses of silver borne before him: with also two great pillars of silver, and his sergeant-at-
20 arms with a great mace of silver gilt . . . his mule, trapped altogether in crimson velvet and gilt stirrups . . . with his cross bearers and pillar bearers also upon great horses trapped with red scarlet . . . having about him four footmen with gilt pole-axes in their hands. And thus he went until he came to Westminister Hall door . . . and [he] went up through

25 the hall into the Chancery. Howbeit he would most commonly stay
awhile at a bar, made for him a little beneath the Chancery, and there
commune sometime with the judges sometime with other persons. And
that done he would repair into the Chancery, sitting there till eleven of
the clock, hearing suitors and determining of divers matters.

> George Cavendish, *The Life and Death of Cardinal Wolsey*, ed.
> R. S. Sylvester, Early English Text Society, 1959

Questions

a What examples of Wolsey's pomp and ostentation are there in this
   extract?
* b 'Wolsey defended his pomp as necessary to create respect for
   authority.' Comment.
c Explain the references to (i) 'the great seal of England' (line 13) (ii)
   'Westminster Hall' (line 16) (iii) 'Chancery' (line 26).
d What kinds of 'divers matters' (line 29) would have been determined
   by Wolsey in Chancery?
* e 'The view which sees him as a layman inadequately disguised under a
   red hat is a dull and false one'. Comment on this assessment of Wolsey
   in the light of this extract.

3 Wolsey and Star Chamber

And for your realm, our lord be thanked, it was never in such peace or
tranquility; for all this summer I have had neither of riot, felony, nor
forcible entry, but that your laws be in every place indifferently
ministered, without leaning of any manner. Albeit, there hath lately, as I
5 am informed, been a fray between Pygot, your sergeant and Sir Andrew
Windsor's servants, for the seisin of a ward whereto they both pretend
titles; in the which fray one man was slain. I trust at the next term to learn
them the law of Star Chamber, that they shall ware how from
thenceforth they shall redress this matter with their hands. They be both
10 learned in the temporal law, and I doubt not good example shall ensue to
see them learn the new law of the Star Chamber, which, God willing they
shall have indifferently ministered to them according to their deserts.

> (1517? 1518?)
> *Letters and Papers, Foreign and Domestic, of the Reign of Henry* VIII
15 *1509–47*, ii, appendix 38

Questions

* a What was 'Star Chamber' at this time?
b What kinds of cases were dealt with in Star Chamber?
c Comment on the phrase 'the new law of the Star Chamber' (line 11).
* d 'I doubt not good example shall ensue. . . .' (line 10). How successful

was Wolsey in his ambition to restore law and order?
* e To what extent did Wolsey's actions in this court contribute to his popularity, and his unpopularity?

4 The 'Amicable Grant' 1525

. . . Now were commissioners sent to the clergy for the fourth part of their land and moveables; and in every assembly the priests answered that they would pay nothing, except it were granted by Convocation; otherwise not. For, they said that never King of England did ask for any
5 man's goods, but by an order of the law; wherefore they said that the cardinal and all the doers thereof were enemies to the king . . . .
When this matter was opened throughout England . . . all people cursed the cardinal and his co-adherents, as subversor of the laws and liberty of England. For they said, if men should give their goods by a
10 commission . . . England should be bond and not free.
. . . Then the cardinal wrote letters to all commissioners of the realm that they should . . . in no wise swerve one jot . . . and every man to be valued according to the valuation taken in the fourteenth year [1522]. This sore touched the city of London, for then the cardinal had promised
15 that whatsoever they valued themselves at, that no man should know it but the king . . . many persons for their more credit and to be the higher esteemed, valued themselves at a greater substance than they were worth. . . . Now was that subtle valuation laid to their charge . . . .
The Duke of Suffolk sat in Suffolk in like commission and by gentle
20 handling caused the rich clothiers to assent and grant the sixth part. . . . They called to them [their workers] and said; Sirs, we be not able to set you a work, our goods be taken from us . . . and men that had no work began to rage and assemble themselves in companies . . . and of [several] towns about, there rebelled four thousand men . . . and began
25 to come together still more. . . . The duke perceiving this began to raise men . . . the gentlemen that were with the duke did so much, that all the bridges were broken, so that their [the rebels] assembly was somewhat letted . . . .
. . . Then the demand of money ceased in all the realm, for well it was
30 perceived the commons would pay none.
Edward Hall, *Chronicle*, ed. C. Whibley, 1904, ii, p 36

Questions

* a Why was there a sudden need for money in 1525?
b What was the basis of the universal objection to Wolsey's exactions?
c Explain the reference to 'the valuation taken in the fourteenth year' (line 13); and comment on the reaction of the city of London.
d What evidence is there here of the *absence* of a noble – commons alliance? How would you account for this?

* *e* (i) 'The failure to collect the Amicable Grant should disprove the idea that there was such a thing as a Tudor Despotism.' (ii) 'Popular opinion had made a significant impact on foreign policy.' Comment on these views of the significance of the failure of 1525.

* *f* Who was Edward Hall? What is his importance as an historian of early Tudor England?

5 Cardinal Wolsey and the Papal Tiara

'The papal tiara hovered in Wolsey's eyes over his own uplifted brow' wrote A. F. Pollard: this yearning after grandeur was 'the simple and straight thread' through the labyrinth of his foreign policy. No attempt to enter that labyrinth will be made here, but a certain amount of
5 evidence will be considered suggesting that Wolsey was not so single-minded in his ambition to become pope as Pollard assumed. Polydore Vergil's comment in 1521 may have been a more pertinent one: that Wolsey's diplomatic simulation exceeded his true ambition . . . .

A cardinal who aspired to become pope should surely pay attention to
10 his own standing in the Roman court and sustain his friends there. But Wolsey on the whole neglected this. Once he had received the red hat he seems to have been content to remain an absentee, although a non-curia cardinal was like 'a fish out of water'. . . . Unlike his predecessor as archbishop of York, Cardinal Bainbridge, Wolsey had no experience of
15 Italian politics and the working of the curia. . . . The French cardinal Georges d'Amboises (d. 1510) . . . who definitely did aspire to be pope, not only visited the curia, but even secured the red hat for a number of his own relatives. Wolsey's influence among the curia cardinals depended on a few superficial courtesies expressed in letters; Lorenzo Campeggio, who
20 was legate in England in 1518 – 19, was the only one with whom he could claim an acquaintance. . . . Cardinal Giulio de' Medici, the pope's cousin, was Protector of England and apparently Wolsey's most eminent agent in the curia . . . .

Wolsey's contacts with Rome depended more upon minor figures
25 than cardinals. . . . Silvestro Gigli (bishop of Worcester) was of considerable personal service . . . [but] Gigli continued to complain that he was kept short of letters from Wolsey and that Leo x himself was troubled by this infrequent communication. . . . His complaints reached their height in a letter of 4 April 1520, reporting papal indignation at being
30 kept in the dark especially when English diplomacy was so active . . . the pope pointed out that other princes wrote even when there was nothing to write about . . . .

While this evidence of a detached attitude towards the court of Rome suggests that Wolsey had no scheme of obtaining the papal tiara for
35 himself, the evidence from the two papal vacancies during his rule also seems, on the whole, to confirm his reluctance. These vacancies followed the deaths of Popes Leo x and Adrian vi . . . .

Wolsey had been flattered by Charles V as a prospective pope, when they met at Bruges in August 1521: but this was before Leo X's death when there were no immediate prospects of a vacancy. The source which most strongly suggests that Wolsey had serious intentions is the account of interviews with him sent by the imperial ambassador De Mesa, bishop of Badajoz, to Charles V. . . . De Mesa nevertheless stated that Wolsey had been under pressure from Henry VIII to put himself forward as a candidate; not that it was his own ambition. . . . Wolsey told De Mesa that he would be glad of the tiara mainly to exalt the emperor and Henry VIII; that after the defeat of the French he would accompany them both on a crusade. This sounds as though he saw the prospect hazily as an expedient which would advance his general policy, but in practice it was little more than a conceit useful in the game of diplomacy . . . .

A more explicit statement of Wolsey's private attitude, unaffected by the need to impress an imperial ambassador is found in a letter of John Clerk (bishop of Bath and Wells) . . . who wrote on 13 January 1522:

. . . I did not gretely labor bifor the Conclave [the College of Cardinals], by cause your Grace at my departyng shewed me precisely that ye wolde never medle therwith. And on my faith, ware not the Kyngs persuasions, I shulde stande yet in greate doubte whether your Grace wollde accepte it or no . . . .

It cannot be established exactly how many votes were cast for Wolsey in each scrutiny of the conclave, as the accounts conflict [ranging from five to nineteen] . . . . Cardinal Petrucci, however, made the following significant comment to Richard Pace [Secretary to Henry VIII, 1516]:

. . . he shewide me that your grace hadde divers voyces in the election by the means of the sayde Cardinal de Medicis and that he hyself was oone of them. Howbeitt the greter numbre wolde nott consent thereunto allegynge that Your Grace wolde nevyr come to Rome. . . .

In the 1523 vacancy Wolsey again sounds a reluctant candidate. Though he made a promise that if elected he would arrive in Rome within three months, he also suggested that Henry VIII would come too. . . . With his instructions to Clerk and Pace, he sent two sets of letters to the cardinals: one recommending de' Medici, the other himself, but the instructions suggest that unless the outlook was very favourable, de' Medici should be urged; meanwhile he wrote to the king that he would rather remain in his service than be ten popes. His absence from the conclave in any case made it even less likely than in 1521 that he would be elected. . . . This is pointed out in a letter (of 14 September 1523).

[We] must shewe your Grace the worst. Many of our corty(ers) and also Cardynalles cannot abyde the heryng that any (one) absent should be chosen, for feare of translatyng the See, and other sondry inconvenyentes . . . .

According to Pollard, Wolsey received no votes at all in that particularly long conclave (1 October to 23 November); but various letters definitely disprove this [the figure of twenty-two votes is ascribed to Wolsey for the scrutiny of 16 October], although there seems to be no account of how the voting went in each of the many scrutinies . . . .

85   Giulio de' Medici was elected Pope Clement VII [and] Wolsey wrote to Rome in terms which suggest relief at the outcome:

> . . . Assuring you that I cannot with my tong or penne exprime the inwarde joye . . . to see hym whom I have so long and so muche lovid honoured and ben so entierly dedicate unto, thus called by God to the supreme place and governance of Cristes religion, being, as I take God to recorde, ferre more
> 90   joyful thereof, then if it had happened uppon myne owne person . . . .

> D. S. Chambers, 'Cardinal Wolsey and the Papal Tiara', *BIHR* 38 (1969) pp 20–30

Questions

a   What evidence is there of Wolsey's 'detached attitude towards the court of Rome' (line 33)?

b   'If his brow was uplifted before the papal tiara it was uplifted with reluctance.' What evidence is there to support this view of Wolsey's attitude towards the papal vacancies in 1521 and 1523?

c   'Wolsey had been flattered by Charles V as a prospective pope. . . . ' (line 38). Comment on English foreign policy at this time in the light of this statement.

* d   If Wolsey had become pope, what might have been the consequences for (i) the church (ii) England?

* e   'To the eminent Tudor historian A. F. Pollard the meaning of Wolsey's diplomacy was clear; it entirely hitched England to the Holy See.' What other interpretations of Wolsey's foreign policy have been put forward?

6 The Diplomatic Revolution

. . . Then after the [French] King's delivery from the emperor's bondage – the King our sovereign lord being security for the recompense of all such demands and restitutions as should be demanded of the French King – the Cardinal lamenting the French king's calamity
5 and the Pope's great adversity (who yet remained in Castel St. Angelo) . . . toiled all that he could with the King and his council to take order as well for the delivery of the one as for the quietness of the other.

Now divers of the great nobles and lords of the council lay in wait with my Lady Anne Boleyn, to espy a convenient time and occasion to take the
10 Cardinal in a snare . . . supposing it best to cause him . . . to travel beyond the seas. . . . They said that it were more meet for his high discretion, wit, and authority, to compass and bring to pass a perfect peace among these great and most mighty princes of the world, than for

any other person within this realm or elsewhere. . . . This matter was so
15 handled that the Cardinal was commanded to prepare himself for this
journey . . . .
 . . . Thus continued the [French] King and my lord in Amiens [9
August] the space of two weeks and more, consulting and feasting each
other divers times. And on the feast of the assumption of Our Lady [18
20 August], my lord rose betimes and went to the cathedral and there before
my lady Regent and the Queen of Navarre he said his service and
mass. . . . The King resorted unto the church . . . and a bishop sang high
mass. And at the fraction of the host, the same bishop divided the
sacrament between the king and the Cardinal, for the performance of the
25 peace concluded between them . . . .
 . . . In the morning that my lord should depart and remove, being
then at mass in his closet, he consecrated the Chancellor of France a
cardinal, and put upon him the habit due to that order. And then he took
his journey towards England . . . . [1527].
   George Cavendish, *The Life and Death of Cardinal Wolsey*, ed.
   R. S. Sylvester, Early English Text Society, 1959

Questions

a Explain the reference to 'the [French] King's delivery from the
   emperor's bondage' (lines 1−2)?
b What was 'the Pope's great adversity' (line 5)?
* c What were (i) the terms of 'the peace concluded between them' (lines
   24−5) (ii) the consequences of this agreement?
d 'He consecrated the Chancellor of France a cardinal' (lines 27−8).
   Comment.
* e 'Now divers of the great nobles and lords of the council lay in
   wait . . . to take the Cardinal in a snare' (lines 8−10). To what extent
   was Wolsey's fall (1529) the product of an aristocratic reaction?

7 Assessments of Wolsey

(a) The Cardinal is the person who rules both the King and the entire
Kingdom. . . . He is about 46, very handsome, learned, extremely
eloquent, of vast ability and indefatigable. He, alone, transacts the same
business as that which occupies all the magistracies, offices and councils of
5 Venice, both civil and criminal, and all state affairs, likewise, are managed
by him, let their nature be what it may. He has the reputation of being
extremely just: he favours the people exceedingly, and especially the
poor; hearing their suits, and seeking to dispatch them instantly; he also
makes the lawyers plead *gratis* for all paupers. He is in very great repute −
10 seven times more so than if he were Pope . . . .
   Sebastian Giustiani, Venetian Ambassador since 1515, in *Calendar
   of State Papers, Venetian* (1519) ii, p 314

(b) Wolsey with his arrogance and ambition aroused against himself the hatred of the whole country, and by his hostility towards the nobility and the common people, caused them the greatest irritation through his vainglory. He was, indeed, detested by everyone, because he assumed
5 that he could undertake nearly all the offices of state by himself. It was, indeed, a fine sight to watch this fellow, untrained in the law, sitting in court and giving judgement. . . . The government of Wolsey at first had a specious appearance of justice for the common people, but this impression quickly disappeared, since it was only a shadow . . . .
10   Polydore Vergil, *Anglica Historia* ed. D. Hay, Camden Society LXXIV (1950) p 230 (This account did not appear in print until the third edition of Vergil's *Historia* in 1555)

(c) Why come ye not to court?
To whyche court?
To the kynges court,
Or to Hampton Court? –
5 Nay, to the Kynges courte:
The Kynges courte
Shulde have the excellence;
But Hampton Court
Hath the preemynence,
10 And Yorkes Place,
With my lordes grace,
To whose magnifycence
Is all the confluence,
Sutys and supplycacyons
15 Embassades of all nacyons
Strawe for Lawe canon
Or for the lawe common,
Or for lawe cyvyll!
It shall be as he wyll.
     John Skelton, *Why come ye not to court?* (1522? 1523?)

Questions

a Compare and contrast the first two extracts; which would you regard as the more accurate?
b What complaints is Skelton making about Wolsey?
c Was John Skelton a reliable witness?
* *d* (i) 'An essentially medieval man in a modern society' (ii) 'The truth is that he stood midway between the old and the new' (iii) 'Wolsey was a Renaissance man'. Which of these verdicts by modern historians would you regard as the most accurate?

III   The Henrician Reformation

Introduction

'The Reformation in England was in two parts. Henry VIII achieved a political revolution in the government of the church by instituting an autonomous English church with himself as supreme head between 1533 and 1534. The movement for religious reformation . . . made slight headway while he was alive . . . .' Thus M. D. Palmer succinctly expresses the dual nature of what, for want of a better phrase, is usually described as the Henrician Reformation.

It is something of a paradox that Henry VIII, a devout catholic, and *Fidei Defensor*, should have been the instrument of a schism which, according to the traditional view, was brought about by his determination to guarantee the succession and the Tudor state.[1]

From 1529 to 1532 pressure was exerted upon the church in England but no legislation was enacted against papal authority; neither was the required divorce secured. It is rather difficult to understand why Henry VIII waited for three years before begining to cut England's ties with Rome.[2] G. R. Elton argues that the delay was because Henry had no coherent policy; and that it was Thomas Cromwell — whose advent to the arena of power coincided with a distinct change in policy — who had to show Henry what to do through the power of statute.[3] In any event, Anne Boleyn was pregnant early in 1533 and the 'King's Private Matter' had to be resolved urgently.

A sequence of truly revolutionary acts of parliament now cut the bonds — spiritual, legal and financial — which linked the English church and state to Rome. The main landmarks were the Act in Restraint of Appeals, 1533 (with its famous preamble); and the Act of Supremacy, 1534, confirming Henry's headship of the church. This latter act explicitly reserved to the Crown the former organising and jurisdictional powers of the papacy in England. Implicitly, as the succeeding years were to demonstrate, the Crown assumed the right to define what the true teaching of the church should be and to control doctrinal issues.

These changes produced very little opposition; though how far the group of risings known as the Pilgrimage of Grace in 1536– 37 were anti-Reformation in origin, is a matter of debate.[4] Few chose to follow the example of Bishop Fisher and Sir Thomas More; and there were, in total, only some forty-five martyrs. The clue to this lack of opposition, it is argued, was that the episcopacy was prepared to accept Henry's schismatic acts, provided there was no change in doctrine or religious practice.

Religious opinion in Tudor England, however, was not to be created by acts of parliament. 'The content of the revolutionary years 1532–40, "the period of Cromwell's ascendency", prove on examination,' writes A. G. Dickens, 'religious as much as legal.' While the government swept away the connection with Rome, and the monasteries, radical groups which were protestant or nearly so, led by Thomas Cromwell and abetted by a half-protestant archbishop of Canterbury, were preparing advances on the liturgical front. The *Ten Articles* of 1536, the first of the Henrician formularies of the faith, reveal a degree of Lutheranism. The semi-official *Bishops Book* of 1537 reflected protestant influences. At the same time, two sets of ecclesiastical injunctions, of 1536 and 1538, began the reform of the new English church.

Not even the conservative reaction of 1539–40, and afterwards, could halt the movement; despite the Six Articles Act, 1539, with its ferocious penalties; the catholic *King's Book* (1543); and an act in the same year limiting, amongst other things, Bible reading to the upper classes. It is clear from Henry VIII's famous last speech of December 1545, with its impassioned plea for charity and concord, that the king was well aware that his experiment in anglo-catholicism might not survive his death.

1 For a contrary view see M. Levine, *Tudor Dynastic Problems* (1973) chapter 3
2 For a lucid discussion of this point see C. S. L. Davies, *Peace, Print and Protestantism* (1976) pp 179–82
3 For Elton's celebrated thesis of the Tudor Revolution in Government inspired by Thomas Cromwell, see his *England under the Tudors* (1974) chapter VII, and especially, appendix 2
4 Compare, for example, A. G. Dickens, *The English Reformation* (1972) pp 122–8; and C. S. L. Davies, op. cit., pp 200–208

Further Reading

D. Pill, *The English Reformation, 1529–58* (1973), and M. D. Palmer, *Henry VIII* (1971) are excellent introductions for students and contain useful bibliographies. A convenient collection of documents is *The Reformation in England to the Accession of Elizabeth I* (1967), edited by A. G. Dickens and D. Carr. Very stimulating and demanding sections are to be found in G. R. Elton, *England under the Tudors* (1974), and *Reform and Reformation* (1977); C. S. L. Davies, *Peace, Print and Protestantism* (1976); C. Russell, *The Crisis of Parliaments* (1971); J. J. Scarisbrick, *Henry VIII* (1968); and C. Cross, *Church and People, 1450–1660* (1976). *Thomas Cromwell and the English Reformation* (1959), by A. G. Dickens, and his *English Reformation* (1972), cannot be neglected by any serious student of the subject.

1 Anticlericalism

To the King our sovereign Lord.

. . . And this most pestilent mischief [poverty] is come upon your said
poor bedesmen by the reason that there is, in the times of your noble
predecessors passed, craftily crept into this your realm another sort (not of
5 impotent, but) of strong, puissant and counterfeit holy, and idle beggars
and vagabonds . . . . These are . . . the bishops, abbots, priors, deacons,
archdeacons, suffragans, priests, monks, canons, friars, pardoners and
summoners. And who is able to number this idle, ravenous sort, which
(setting all labour aside) have begged so importunately that they have
10 gotten into their hands more than the third part of all your realm. The
goodliest lordships, manors, lands and territories are theirs. Besides this
they have the tenth part of all the corn, meadow, pasture, grass, wool,
colts, calves, lambs, pigs, geese and chickens. Over and besides, the tenth
part of every servant's wages, the tenth part of the wool, milk, honey
15 wax, cheese and butter. Yea, and they look so narrowly upon their profits
that the poor wives must be accountable to them of every tenth egg, or
else she . . . shall be taken as an heretic . . . . What money pull they in
by probates of testaments, privy tithes, and by men's offerings to their
pilgrimages and at their first masses? Every man and child that is buried,
20 must pay somewhat for masses and dirges to be sung for him . . . . What
money get they by mortmains, by hearings of confessions . . . by
hallowing of churches . . . by cursing of men, and absolving them again
for money? . . . Finally the infinite number of friars; what get they in a
year? . . . .
25 What remedy: make laws against them? I am in doubt whether ye be
able: are they not stronger in your own parliament house than yourself?
What a number of bishops, abbots and priors are lords of your
parliament? . . . What laws can be made against them? . . . Who is he
(though he be grieved never so sore) . . . dare lay it to their charge by any
30 way of action? And if he do, then is he . . . accused of heresy . . . . He
shall be excommunicate, and then be all his actions dashed. So captive are
your laws unto them that no man that they list to excommunicate may be
admitted to sue any action in any of your courts. If any man in your
sessions dare be so hardy to indict a priest of any such crime, he
35 hath . . . such a yoke of heresy laid in his neck, that it maketh him wish
that he had not done it . . . . Had not Richard Hunne commenced action
of praemunire against a priest, he had been yet alive, and none heretic at
all, but an honest man . . . .

Simon Fish, *A Supplicacyon for the Beggars*, 1528–9, ed. F. J.
Furnivall, Early English Text Society, 1871, extra series, xiii, pp
1–15

Questions

* *a* Who was Simon Fish? Comment on the timing of his plea to Henry
VIII.

b What charges are levelled against the clergy by Fish?
c What obstacles are there to the redress of grievances against the clergy?
d Explain the reference to Richard Hunne (line 36).

2 Act for the Pardon of the Clergy 1531

The King, our Sovereign Lord, calling to his blessed and most gracious remembrance that his good and loving subjects the most reverend father in God the Archbishop of Canterbury and other bishops suffragans, prelates and other spiritual persons of the province of the archbishopric of
5 Canterbury . . . and the ministers . . . which have exercised, practised or executed in spiritual courts and other spiritual jurisdictions within the said province, have fallen and incurred into divers changes of his laws by things done, perpetrated and committed contrary to the order of his laws, and specially contrary to the four of the Statutes of Provisors, Provisions
10 and Praemunire. . . . His Highness . . . by authority of his Parliament, hath given and granted his liberal and free pardon to his said good and loving spiritual subjects . . . .
        22 Hen. VIII, c. 15: *Statutes of the Realm*, iii, 334—8

Questions

* *a* What was the background to the passing of this legislation?
  b Explain the reference to the Statutes of Provisors, Provisions and Praemunire (lines 9—10).
  c Identify the archbishop of Canterbury referred to in line 3.
* *d* What was the consequence of this statute for (i) the province of Canterbury (ii) the province of York?

3 The Supplication of the Commons against the Ordinaries 1532

1 First, the prelates and other of the clergy of this your realm, being your subjects, in their Convocation by them holden . . . have made and daily make divers fashions of laws and ordinaries concerning temporal things, and some of them be repugnant to the laws and statutes of your
5 realm; not having ne requiring your most royal assent to the same laws by them so made, nor any assent or knowledge of your lay subjects is had to the same, nor to them published and known in the English tongue . . . .
2 Also divers and many of your said most humble and obedient subjects, and especially those of the poorest sort . . . be daily converted
10 and called before the said spiritual ordinaries . . . for displeasure without any provable cause . . . and sometime they be committed to prison without bail . . . and there some lie . . . half a year . . . .

3 Also your said most humble and obedient subjects find themselves grieved with the great and excessive fees . . . taken in the spiritual
15 courts . . . . Also in probate of testaments . . . there is . . . long delays . . . .
4 And also the said spiritual ordinaries do daily confer and give sundry benefits unto certain young folks . . . whereby the said ordinaries do keep and detain . . . the profits . . . in their own hands . . . .
        Public Record Office, SP 61, no. 22

Questions

*   a   Comment on the origins of the 'Supplication'.
    b   Explain the meaning in this context of 'Ordinaries'.
    c   Analyse the complaints set out above.
*   d   What were the immediate consequences of this 'Supplication'?

4   Act in conditional Restraint of Annates 1532

Forasmuch as it is well perceived, by long-approved experience, that great and inestimable sums of money have been daily conveyed out of this realm, to the impoverishment of the same; and especially such sums of money as the Pope's Holiness, his predecessors, and the court of Rome,
5 by long time have heretofore taken from all and singular those spiritual persons which have been named, elected, presented or postulated to be archbishops or bishops, within this realm of England, under the title of the annates, otherwise called first fruits: which annates or first fruits, heretofore have been taken of every archbishopric or bishopric within
10 this realm, by restraint of the Pope's bulls for confirmations . . . or other things requisite and necessary to the attaining of those their promotions; and have been compelled to pay, before they could attain the same, great sums of money . . . And because the said annates have risen, grown, and increased . . . against all equity and justice . . . .
15 It is therefore ordained and established, by authority of this present Parliament, that the unlawful payments of annates, or first fruits, and all manner of contributions for the same, for any archbishopric or bishopric . . . shall from henceforth utterly cease . . . other or otherwise than hereafter in this present act is declared . . . .
20 And forasmuch as the King's Highness and this his High Court of Parliament, neither have, nor do intend to use in this, or any other like cause, any manner of extremity or violence, before gentle courtesy and friendly ways and means first approved and attempted . . . have therefore thought convenient to commit the final order and determination of
25 the premises, in all things, unto the King's Highness . . . .
        23 Hen. VIII, c. 20: *Statutes of the Realm*, iii, 385–8

Questions

a Comment on the claim that 'great and inestimable sums of money' (line 2) have left England for Rome.

b How had English ecclesiastics been made to pay annates or first fruits?

c What evidence is there of a conciliatory tone in this document?

* *d* When, why, and with what consequences for the church, was this 'conditional' act made 'absolute'?

5 Act in Restraint of Appeals 1533

Where by divers sundry old authentic histories and chronicles, it is manifestly declared and expressed that this realm of England is an empire, and so hath been accepted in the world, governed by one Supreme Head and King, having the dignity and royal estate of the imperial Crown of
5 the same, unto whom a body politic . . . divided in terms, and by names of spiritualty and temporalty, be bounden and owe to bear, next to God, a natural and humble obedience . . . .

And whereas the King, his most noble progenitors . . . made sundry ordinances, laws, statutes and provisions for the entire and sure
10 conservation of the prerogatives . . . of the said imperial Crown of this realm, and of the jurisdictions spiritual and temporal of the same to keep it free from the annoyance as well of the see of Rome, as from the authority of other foreign potentates . . . .

And notwithstanding . . . sundry inconveniences and dangers . . .
15 have risen and sprung by reason of appeals sued out of this realm to the see of Rome, in causes testamentary, causes of matrimony and divorces, right of titles . . . not only to the great inquietation, vexation, trouble, costs and charges of the King's Highness and many of his subjects . . . but also to the great delay and let to the true and speedy determination of the
20 said causes . . . .

In consideration whereof the King's Highness, his nobles and Commons . . . enact . . . that all [such] causes shall be from henceforth heard, examined, discussed, clearly, finally, and definitively adjudged and determined within the King's jurisdiction and authority and not
25 elsewhere . . . .

24 Hen. VIII, c. 12: *Statutes of the Realm*, iii, 427–9

Questions

a What were the objectives of this act of March 1533?

b What were its immediate consequences?

* *c* 'This Act was not the "breach with Rome".' Comment.

* *d* 'The essential ingredient of the Tudor revolution was the concept of national sovereignty . . . . The critical term (in the preamble) is "empire".' Consider G. R. Elton's view of the significance of the preamble to this statute.

6 An Act for the Establishment of the King's Succession 1534

... We your said most humble and obedient subjects . . . calling to our remembrance the great divisions which in times past hath been in this realm by reason of several titles pretended to the imperial crown of the same . . . whereof hath ensued great effusion and destruction of man's
5 blood . . . And the greatest occasion thereof hath been because no perfect and substantial provision by law hath been made within this realm of itself when doubts and questions have been moved . . . of the certainty and legality of the succession and posterity of the Crown; By reason whereof the bishop of Rome and See Apostolic, contrary to the great and
10 inviolable grants of jurisdiction given by God immediately to emperors, kings and princes in succession to their heirs, hath presumed in times past to invest who should please them to inherit in other men's kingdoms and dominions . . . .

In consideration whereof your said most humble and obedient subjects
15 the nobles and commons of this realm . . . do therefore most humbly beseech your Highness . . . that the marriage solemnised between your highness and the Lady Catherine, being before lawful wife to Prince Arthur your elder brother, which by him was carnally known, as doth duly appear by sufficient proof in a lawful process had and made before
20 Thomas, by the sufferance of God now archbishop of Canterbury and metropolitan primate of all this realm [at Dunstable, 23 May 1533]; shall be by authority of this present Parliament . . . deemed utterly void and annulled . . . . And that the lawful matrimony had and solemnised between your Highness and your most dear and entirely beloved wife
25 Queen Anne shall be established . . . according to the just judgement of the said Thomas, archbishop of Canterbury [at Lambeth, 28 May 1533] . . . .

And for the more sure establishment of the succession of your most royal Majesty according to the tenor and form of this act [the heirs of
30 Henry and Anne] . . . all the nobles of your realm spiritual and temporal as all other your subjects . . . shall make a corporal oath . . . that they shall truly . . . keep . . . the whole effects and contents of this present act . . . . And if any persons . . . obstinately refuse that to do . . . then every person so doing to be taken and accepted for offender in misprision
35 of high treason . . . .

25 Hen. VIII, c. 22: *Statutes of the Realm*, iii, 471 – 4

Questions

a Contrast the reference to the pope in the preamble with that in the Conditional Act of Annates, 1532 (extract 4). How would you account for the difference?

b Comment on the method by which the 'King's Great Matter' was finally resolved.

*   *c*   How did this act contribute to the deaths of Bishop Fisher and Sir
Thomas More?

7   The Act of Supremacy 1534

Albeit the King's Majesty justly and rightly is and oweth to be the
Supreme Head of the Church of England, and so is recognised by the
clergy of this realm in their Convocations . . . be it enacted . . . that the
King or Sovereign Lord . . . shall be . . . the only Supreme Head on
5   earth of the Church in England . . . and . . . shall have full power and
authority from time to time to visit, repress, redress, reform, order,
correct, restrain, and amend all such errors, heresies, abuses, offences,
contempts and enormities . . . to the pleasure of Almighty God, the
increase of virtue in Christ's religion, and for the conservation of the
10   peace, unity and tranquillity of this realm; any usage, custom, foreign
laws, foreign authority, prescription, or any other thing or things to the
contrary hereof notwithstanding.
26 Hen. VIII, c. I: *Statutes of the Realm*, iii, 492

Questions

a   Comment on the kings's title set out in line 2.
b   What powers were given to the king by this act?
*   *c*   'He had none of the spiritual powers of the Pope.' Comment on this
assessment of Henry's powers after 1534.
*   *d*   What part was played by 'the clergy of this realm in their
Convocations' (line 3) in the making of the political Reformation?

8   The Act of the Six Articles 1539

First, that in the most blessed sacrament of the altar . . . is present really,
under the form of bread and wine, the natural body and blood of our
Saviour Jesus Christ . . . and that after the consecration there remaineth
no substance of bread or wine, nor any other substance but the substance
5   of Christ, God and man.
Secondly, that communion in both kinds is not necessary . . . to all
persons . . . .
Thirdly, that priests . . . may not marry by the law of God.
Fourthly, that vows of chastity or widowhood . . . ought to be observed
10   by the law of God . . . .
Fifthly, that it is meet and necessary that private masses be continued and
admitted in this the King's English Church and Congregation . . . .
Sixthly, that auricular confession is expedient and necessary to be retained
and continued . . . .
15   Any who . . . declare anything contrary to the first article, or who

'despise the said blessed sacrament' shall . . . be guilty of heresy and burned.

Any who preach or teach . . . contrary to the other five articles . . . shall suffer a felon's death.

31 Hen. VIII, c. 14: *Statutes of the Realm*, iii, 742–3

Questions

a Identify the main points of catholic dogma which are set out in the Six Articles.

* b 'Couched in conservative, not to say reactionary terms'. Comment on this view of the Six Articles.
* c How effective was this act in practice?
* d What other attempts were made to determine dogma from 1536 to the death of Henry VIII?

9 Catholic Reaction 1543: an Act for the Advancement of True Religion

. . . Recourse must be had to the Catholic and Apostolic Church for the decision of controversies; and therefore all books of the Old and New Testaments in English, being of Tyndal's false translation, or comprising any matter of Christian religion, articles of the faith, or Holy Scripture,
5 contrary to the doctrine set forth since Anno Dom. 1540, or to be set forth by the King, shall be abolished. No printer or bookseller shall utter any of the aforesaid books. No person shall play in interlude, sing, or rhyme, contrary to the said doctrine. No person shall retain any English books or writings concerning matter against the holy and blessed
10 sacrament of the altar, or for the maintenance of anabaptists, or other books abolished by the King's proclamation. There shall be no annotations or preambles in Bibles or New Testaments in English. The Bible shall not be read in English in any church. No women or artificers, prentices, journeymen, serving men of the degree of yeomen or under,
15 husbandmen, nor labourers, shall read the New Testament in English. Nothing shall be taught or maintained contrary to the King's instructions. And if any spiritual person preach, teach, or maintain anything contrary to the King's instructions or determinations, made or to be made, he shall for his first offence recant, for his second abjure and bear a
20 fagot, and for his third shall be adjudged an heretic, and be burned and lose all his goods and chattels.

34 *Henry VIII, c. 1, Statutes at Large*

Questions

a How wide-spread had Bible reading become by 1543?
b Explain the reference to 'Tyndal's false translation' (line 3).

c 'The Bible shall not be read in English in any church' (lines 12−13). Why not?

* *d* Was this legislation likely to have the desired effect?

10 The Royal Divorce: Occasion or Cause?

The place of the royal divorce in the history of the Reformation will always remain a subject for argument. Protestant writers have tended to dismiss it as a mere 'occasion' rather than a genuine cause; Catholics have sometimes regarded the divorce as the chief cause of the cataclysm and
5 supposed that, had it not been pressed, England might well have remained a Catholic nation. To the present writer neither of these views seems wholly acceptable. The Protestants have too readily assumed the inevitability of a Reformation similar in timing and in character to the one which actually occurred. The divorce was something more than a
10 mere 'occasion'; without it the schism would not have been consummated by 1533−4. Had Henry either abandoned or obtained his divorce he would most likely have tried, and with success, to hold his realm in some sort of spiritual allegiance to Rome, though it seems inconceivable that he or his people would tamely have reverted to any
15 earlier situation. We may well agree with Pollard that the Pope's refusal of the divorce 'alienated the only power which might have kept in check the anti-papal and anti-sacerdotal tendencies then growing up in England.'
On the other side we must avoid the temptation to equate the
20 Henrician Schism with the Protestant Reformation. The divorce suit did not create either Protestantism or those anti-papal and anti-sacerdotal forces which smoothed its path. That such forces were diverse in origin and deep-laid in society . . . (and) that by the thirties they had reached a critical intensity throughout the dominant classes and regions of England
25 cannot be doubted. And so far as the new beliefs are concerned, it must be acknowledged that, irrespective of his relations with Rome, Henry VIII could not have frozen the English in their religious posture of the year 1530. Even during the last seven years of his reign, when he was attempting to check Protestantism, it was spreading more rapidly than
30 ever before, and it captured the government immediately upon his death. When we are tempted to underestimate its expansive capacities, we should recall that in the Netherlands, in Scotland and elsewhere, it soon played havoc with the plans of Kings and governments. At the death of Henry VIII Calvinism still lay, so far as England was concerned, in the
35 womb of the future; but its new challenge, politically more formidable than that of Lutheranism, was bound to be made some day, whatever the complexion of future English governments. Moreover, the special attractions of Protestantism for the ruling classes rapidly manifested themselves; Henry VIII was not immortal and a strong chance remained
40 that future rulers of England would be captured by Protestant beliefs. The

most knowledgeable among us cannot speculate with much profit regarding the probable courses of history, had the divorce problem been solved in Rome or had it never presented itself. Yet was the divorce anything more than one of the many dangerous reefs which English
45 Catholicism had to circumnavigate? And English Catholicism, despite its gilded decorations, was an old, unseaworthy and ill-commanded galleon, scarcely able to continue its voyage without the new seamen and shipwrights produced (but produced far too late in the day) by the Counter-Reformation.
50 Over and above these considerations, the divorce and its attendant schism arose from a European pattern destined to persist for another century − a pattern which continually set English nationalism at loggerheads with English Catholicism and which at any stage was liable to plunge the latter into disaster. This pattern consisted of a powerful Spain,
55 seeking not only to curb the Atlantic enterprises of the north-European peoples but to control the Mediterranean, the Italian peninusula and with them a reluctant but often rather powerless Papacy. In that age political and religious controls could not be kept apart, and one finds it impossible to imagine a people as tough, as active and as independent as the Tudor
60 English acquiescing for any length of time in a Christendom organised along these Habsburg lines. In some sense, national schisms like that of England became more possible from 1503, when Spain overran the kingdom of Naples and began to establish its long dominance over central Italy. Even if Henry VIII had remained a model of matrimonial
65 respectability, even if the ministers of Edward VI had been converted by a stray Jesuit, even if Queen Mary had survived for another decade, it still requires a vivid imagination to envisage the English as dutiful children of the Holy See at the end of the century. And among the many forbidding obstacles, Philip II and Calvin are the two which first catch the eye.

A. G. Dickens, *The English Reformation*, 1972, pp 154−6

Questions

a Using this extract as a starting point, discuss Voltaire's remark that 'England separated herself from the Pope because Henry the Eighth fell in love'.

* b What steps did Henry take 'during the last seven years of his reign . . . to check Protestantism' (lines 28−9)? What evidence is there that 'it was spreading more rapidly than ever before' (line 29)?

c What does Dickens mean by the 'special attractions of Protestantism for the ruling classes' which 'rapidly manifested themselves' (lines 37−9)?

* d 'Protestantism . . . captured the government immediately upon his [Henry VIII] death' (lines 29−30). How would you explain this development?

IV   A study in depth: The Dissolution of the Monasteries 1536—40

Introduction

The dissolution of the monasteries was a revolution in land ownership second only to that which followed the Norman Conquest. Possibly because it is one of the best documented episodes in Tudor history it has generated a whole series of debates amongst historians who have been concerned with problems such as the causes of the dissolution, or rather dissolutions of 1536 and subsequently; the impact on the land market of the sale of monastic property; and the social, or other, consequences of the latter. A related problem is the connection, if any, between the dissolution and the rebellions and unrest of 1536—7.

An earlier generation of historians saw the dissolution as the essential concomitant of the Henrician Reformation. Their view was that once Henry VIII had assumed the Supreme Headship of the Church then monastic communities represented a political threat to the crown as cells of papal cancer in need of excision. This operation was successfully carried out between 1536 and 1540, after hastily conducted royal visitations of the monasteries, often inconsistent with a conscientious handling of the evidence, had provided sufficient excuse that the inhabitants were no longer fulfilling their vows. The enforced sale by the crown of vast amounts of monastic property, at far less than its real market value, the greater part of it by 1547, was poor economics but politically a master stroke ensuring the permanence of the Henrician Reformation by the simple expedient of selling shares in it. Those who had purchased monastic property now had a 'vested interest' in its continuation. The dissolution was, in effect, and probably in intention, a gigantic bribe to the laity to induce them to acquiesce in the revolution effected by Henry VIII. From the very beginning of the Reformation Parliament there had been those who had 'thirsted for land wherewith to make themselves gentlemen', and one consequence of the suppression of the monasteries was to be the creation of a new and politically ambitious landed class, the 'gentry', whose economic basis was to be their careful management of medium-sized estates of which ex-monastic property formed a major portion.

Research over the past quarter of a century has altered this picture at practically every point. The dissolution is now seen as neither an integral, nor an essential, part of the Henrician Reformation in England and Wales. Indeed, it is argued, it might well have taken place if there had been no breach with Rome at all and it might well have remained final even if that breach had been healed by Henry VIII himself or Mary Tudor. By no stretch of the imagination can the monasteries be regarded as representing a political challenge to the royal supremacy. Though a high proportion of those who were executed for refusing to accept Henry's supremacy were monks and friars they were, in total, only a mere handful who belonged to the Carthusian and Reformed Franciscan orders, both renowned for their rigorous observance. In any event, would dissolution have been the right way to deal with the politically disaffected? Would dissolution and the dispersal of the monks have induced papally-orientated monks to be any more loyal to the regime which dispossessed them? (In fact, one of the consequences of dissolution was to drive some of the dispossessed religious into association with the northern rebels in the Pilgrimage of Grace). Dissolution was, therefore, more likely to create than to remove opposition to the royal headship.

It is now known that the enforced sale of monastic land did not have the effect of depressing land values; and to argue that by selling off the property of the monasteries Henry VIII created a class with a 'vested interest' in the Reformation is now seen as a misconception. Those members of the Commons in Mary's third parliament who were ready enough to restore the royal supremacy, nevertheless refused to entertain any proposals for the restoration of the properties of the religious orders. In doing this they were not necessarily displaying their protestant sympathies, but their good business sense, into which considerations of faith did not enter. Among the biggest buyers of monastic lands are to be found as frequently those who later became recusants as those who became puritans. It is now almost a truism that conservatism in matters of religion was no bar to the acquisition and retention of monastic lands.

The emergence of the 'gentry' as the dominant class may to some extent have been assisted by the acquisition of additional monastic acres in the 1540s, and later, which clearly helped to change the balance of social groups; but this is not the whole story. It can be argued that the transfer to the crown of the monastic estates delayed, rather than accelerated, the emergence of the gentry as a political force by deferring the day when the crown's financial dependence upon parliamentary grants gave the gentry their political opportunity.

Further Reading

'Traditional' interpretations include A. F. Pollard, *Henry VIII* (1902), and A. D. Innes, *England under the Tudors* (1905). G. R. Elton in *Reform and Reformation* (1977) lucidly summarises what is now known about the topic. A valuable summary of scholarly findings with illustrative documents is Joyce Youings, *The Dissolution of the Monasteries* (1971). See also G. W. O. Woodward, *The Dissolution of the Monasteries* (1966), with selected documentary material; and Geoffrey Baskerville, *English Monks* and the Suppression of the Monasteries (1937). A. G. Dickens and D. Carr, Reformation in England to the Accession of Elizabeth I (1967), contains a documentary section on the dissolution; whilst A. G. Dickens, The English Reformation (1972) has a stimulating section on the topic. The classic work by M. D. Knowles, The Religious Orders in England, III, The Tudor Age (1959) has recently been re-issued in an abbreviated and illustrated form as Bare Ruined Choirs (1977). For the relationship between the Pilgrimage of Grace and the dissolution see C. S. L. Davies, 'The Pilgrimage of Grace reconsidered', Past and Present, 41 (1968); and Anthony Fletcher, Tudor Rebellions (1968).

I The Valor Ecclesiasticus 1535

On 3 November 1534 parliament passed, as well as the Act of Supremacy, the First Fruits and Tenths Act (26 Henry VIII, c. 3) which imposed on the clergy both secular and monastic a tax of one tenth of their net annual income as well as making over to the crown the whole of
5   the first year's income from any new ecclesiastical appointment. Commissioners were appointed comprising the bishop and local gentlemen on 30 January 1535 to make a nationwide inquiry into the true annual value of each ecclesiastical benefice and 'abbey, monastery, priory, and house religious and conventual, as well charter-houses (Carthusian)
10 and others'. It would be a safe assumption that at this time no one in England knew how many monasteries there were in existence, their geographical location and least of all the value of their landed and spiritual revenues. Detailed instructions were prepared in the form of question-naires and on the completion of their inquiries (which was not until the
15 autumn) the commissioners were instructed to prepare 'a fair book of the auditor's fashion', that is a valuation showing the extent and source of gross income, less allowable deductions. The inquiry revealed that in 1535 the total annual income of all the religious orders was somewhere in the region of £160,000 to £200,000 or about three quarters as much
20 again as the average annual income of the crown at the same date.

An Extract from the 'Valor Ecclesiasticus': the Royal Commissioners' Valuation of the Resources of Walsingham Priory[1] in 1535

Priory or Monastery of Walsingham Richard Vowell prior there
It is valued in SPRITUALITIES IN THE COUNTY OF NORFOLK

5   Rectory of All Souls in Great Walsingham and the
rectory of St. Peter's there, as well as the rectory of
All Souls in Little Walsingham, with the priors
tithes (£3) there,   £59. 10s. 5d.
Tithes of wheat sheaves appertaining to the church of
10   Walton,   £2
                                    (Total) £61. 10s. 5d.

	Manor of Great Ryburgh, valued in rents and farms p.a.,	£32. 14s.	7⅞d.
15	Farm of the grain mill there,		113s. 4d.
	Sale of wood in an average year,		76s.
	Profits of the Court there in an average year,		8s. 8d.
	In all	£42. 12s.	7⅞d.
	Manor of Little Ryburgh Woodall, valued in rents		
20	and farms p.a.,	£4. 19s.	4¾d.
	Sale of wood in an average year,		14s. 9d.
	In all	£5. 14s.	1¾d.
	(Twelve more manors and odd rents follow)		
	(Total)	£446. 14s.	5⅝d.

25   DEDUCTED OR ALLOWED ACCORDING TO THE STATUTE
(OF FOUNDATION)

	Sinodals paid:	(in all)	6s. 8d.
	Procurations paid:	(in all)	30s. 6d.
	Annual pensions paid:	(in all)	54s. 3d.

30 Distributed of old at Houghton St. Giles for the soul of William Lexham esquire by the founder's provion, 13s. 4d. Given of old to certain poor men out of the manor of Peterston by the provision of the founder, King Henry VI, 17s. 4d. Distributed to poor men at Bedingham at the feasts of St. Mary and on Perasceves Day for the souls of Edward I, Edward II and 35 John Uvedale, knight, by the founder's provision, 12s. 6d.

		(In all)	43s. 2d.
	Stipends, etc.	(In all) £13.	13s. 4d.
	Rents paid	(Total) £23.	19s. 11½d.
	Fees (to various bailiffs)	(Total) £10.	15s.
40		(Total) £55.	2s. 10½d.
	And there remains clear per annum	£391.	11s. 7¾d.
	The tenth of this is	£39.	3s. 2d.

Also, (belonging to) the prior of Walsingham there is valued in

OFFERINGS

45	In the chapel of the Blessed Virgin Mary last year £250.	0s.	12d.
	To the Holy Milk of the Blessed Virgin Mary		
	there the same year,	42s.	3d.
	In the chapel of St. Laurence the same year, £8.	9s.	1½d.
	(In all) £260.	12s.	4d.
50	of which the tenth is £26.	0s.	15d. (sic)

Valor Ecclesiasticus, Record Commission edition, 1810–34, Vol III, pp 385–8

1 The priory was dissolved on 4 August 1538; the shrine had been dismantled on 14 July.

Questions

a What questions must have been asked by the commissioners in order to produce the answers given?

b What proportion of the priory's total income came from (i) spiritual sources (ii) temporal sources (iii) offerings at the shrine of the Blessed Virgin Mary?

c What was the net annual income of the priory and how was this figure determined?

d The *Valor Ecclesiasticus* included the proportion of total income which the monasteries were legally obliged to devote to charitable expenditure; the national average was less than 2·5 per cent. (i) What was the figure for Walsingham? (ii) Does the low national average figure mean that the lot of the poor cannot have been considerably worsened by the dissolution of the monasteries? (iii) 'In the north parts much of the relief of the commons was by succour of abbeys' (Robert Aske). Comment.

* e 'Whatever its future utility may have been there is no justification whatsoever for regarding the *Valor Ecclesiasticus* as anything more than a taxation assessment.' Do you agree?

2 The Royal Visitation of the Monasteries 1535–6

At the same time as the compilation of the *Valor Ecclesiasticus*, Thomas Cromwell was making use of the powers which had been conferred on him when in January 1535 he had become Vicar General, or the king's vicegerent in·matters spiritual. Making use of the duty placed upon the
5 crown by the Act of Supremacy 1534 (26 Henry VIII, c. 1) 'to visit, repress, redress, reform . . .' the church, he appointed deputies (not local men on this occasion) who were to visit as many religious houses as they could in the time available. The king's visitors began their work in the south and west in the late summer of 1535 and ended in the north in
10 February 1536 – the same month in which the final session of the Reformation Parliament (4 February to 14 April) began.

The work of these visitors has been condemned as worthless by many historians because of the speed of the inquiry. The northern visitation was carried out by Richard Layton and Thomas Legh who, between 22
15 December 1535 and 28 February 1536, a period of two months and six days, claimed to have reported on more than 120 religious houses scattered over a wide area at an average of nearly two visits a day. Their *Compendium Compertorum* or 'Book of Findings' has been regarded as of dubious value.

20 In defence of the visitors, however, recent authorities have suggested that when their findings are compared with those of two other sets of contemporary reports, earlier and admittedly more favourable bishops'

visitations and those of the suppression commissioners after 1536, then
their results are not by any means as unacceptable as has been claimed.
25 In any event, even if the conventional view be accepted – that their
mission was really to gather sufficient evidence to condemn the religious
in the eyes of parliament – for the testimony of the king's visitors to have
been at all credible to contemporaries, the religious must have had no
very outstanding reputation for virtue to begin with. Unfortunately the
30 monasteries were judged as a whole by the excesses which the few
permitted; and in an increasingly secular age there was widespread lack of
public sympathy for the religious ideal.

St Edmund's Monastery at Bury, November 1535

Please it your mastership forasmuch as I suppose ye shall have suit made
unto you touching Bury ere we return, I thought convenient to advertise
you of our proceedings there and also of the compertes of the same. As for
the abbot, we found nothing suspect as touching his living, but it was
5 detected that he lay much forth in his granges, that he delighted much in
playing at dice and cards, and therein spent much money, and in building
for his pleasure. He did not preach openly. Also that he converted divers
farms into copyholds, whereof poor men doth complain. Also he
seemeth to be addicted to the maintaining of such superstitious cer-
10 emonies as hath been used heretofore.

As touching the convent, we could get little or no reports among them,
although we did use much diligence in our examination, and thereby,
with some other arguments gathered of their examinations, I firmly
believe and suppose that they had conferred and compacted before our
15 coming that they should disclose nothing. And yet it is confessed and
proved, that there was here such frequence of women coming and
resorting to this monastery as to no place more. Amongst the relics we
found much vanity and superstition, as the coals that Saint Laurence was
toasted with all, the paring of S. Edmund's nails, S. Thomas of
20 Canterbury's penknife and his boots and divers skulls for the headache;
pieces of the holy cross able to make a whole cross of; other relics for rain
and certain other superstitious usages, for avoiding of weeds growing in
corn, with such other. Here depart of them that be under age upon an
eight, and of them that be above age upon a five would depart if they
25 might, and they be of the best sort in the house and of best learning and
judgement. The whole number of the convent before we came was lx.
saving one, beside iii that were at Oxford. Of Ely I have written to your
mastership by my fellow Richard a Lee. And thus Almighty God have
you in his tuition. From Bury, v. November (1535).
30   Your servant most bounden,
                                                JOHN AP RICE.
John Ap Rice to Secretary Cromwell, *Letters relating to the
Suppression of the Monasteries*, ed. Thomas Wright, Camden
Society, 1843, pp 85–6

Questions

a Why has John Ap Rice decided to write to Cromwell at this time?
b 'Their principal task was to gather material designed to bring celibacy and relics into disrepute and the religious orders with them.' What evidence is there is in this letter to support this view of the visitors' main aims?
c On what sorts of evidence does Rice base his statements? Does his case carry conviction?
* d What motives have been ascribed by historians to Thomas Cromwell in ordering this visitation?

3 Dissolution by Statute

At some point very early in 1536 or possibly late in 1535 the decision was taken, probably on financial grounds, to proceed with the 'resumption' or confiscation of the landed endowments of some of the houses of the regular clergy. The problem was two-fold: which? and how? In the event the Crown shrank from making subjective judgements, and avoided trying to decide the future of each house on its merits or demerits, and introduced a statute which drew certain lines of demarcation though these were shot through with inconsistencies. The act did not provide for dissolution in so many words but the clear assumption was that, deprived of their lands, the religious communities would disappear and this is what in fact happened.

The total number of monasteries actually suppressed totalled some 243 or approximately three out of every ten religious houses throughout the country.[1] Not all the houses which should technically have been dissolved were: between seventy and eighty or more than one fifth of those which 'qualified' were exempted (although only fifty one in the end received patents) under section XIII of the statute which gave the Crown discretion to exempt certain houses by letters patent under the great seal from the operation of the act. A great deal of attention has been focused on this 'exemption' clause. It has been seen as an attempt to solve the 'accommodation problem' created by the large number of religious − 70 per cent of the inhabitants of seventy eight houses in the six counties for which the evidence survives − who wished to exercise their option under the statute to remain in the cloister, by transferring to another house, (though when the act was formulated the magnitude of this problem could hardly have been forseen). Significant inferences have been drawn from the very inclusion in the statute of the option to transfer itself. If the 1536 Act was merely the first stage in a planned total dissolution then it would hardly have been worthwhile to provide alternative accommodation; it would have been simpler (but not cheaper) to provide a pension without option (as was done between 1538−40). The presence of an option clause, it has been argued, seems to indicate therefore that no more than a partial dissolution was intended in 1536.

Alternative interpretations are that the government anticipated large 'fines' for exemptions (and £6000 was actually paid in this way between 1536–8); or that the 'exemption' clause is best explained as a way of retaining some freedom of action for the crown, even a way of retreat if there should be undue popular opposition to the whole process of dissolution.

1   In 1530 there were at least 825 religious houses in England and Wales: 502 monasteries, 136 nunneries, and 187 friaries, containing 7,500 men and 1,800 women, or one in 375 of the total population

The Suppression Act of 1536 — Preamble

An act whereby all religious houses of monks, canons and nuns which may not dispend manors lands tenements and hereditaments above the clear yearly value of £200 are given to the King's Highness, his heirs and successors for ever.

5   Forasmuch as manifest sin, vicious carnal and abominable living, is daily used and committed amongst the little and small abbeys, priories and other religious houses of monks, canons and nuns, where the congregation of such religious persons is under the number of twelve persons, whereby the governors of such religious houses and their
10 convents spoil, destroy, consume and utterly waste, as well their churches, monasteries, priories, principal houses, farms, granges, lands, tenements and hereditaments, as the ornaments of their churches and their goods and chattels, to the high displeasure of Almighty God, slander of good religion and to the great infamy of the King's Highness and the
15 realm if redress should not be had thereof: and albeit that many continual visitations hath been heretofore had by the space of two hundreds years and more, for an honest and charitable reformation of such unthrifty, carnal and abominable living, yet nevertheless little or none amendment is hitherto had, but their vicious living shamelessly increaseth and
20 augmenteth, and by a cursed custom so rooted and infested that a great multitude of the religious persons in such small houses do rather choose to rove abroad in apostacy than to conform them to the observation of good religion; so that without such small houses be utterly suppressed and the religious persons therein committed to great and honourable monasteries
25 of religion in this realm, where they may be compelled to live religiously for reformation of their lives, there can else be no reformation in this behalf: IN CONSIDERATION whereof the King's most royal Majesty being supreme head in earth under God of the Church of England, daily finding and devising the increase, advancement and exaltation of true
30 doctrine and virtue in the said Church, to the only glory and honour of God and the total extirpation and destruction of vice and sin, having

knowledge that the premises be true, as well by the comperta of his late visitations as by sundry credible informations, considering also that divers and great solemn monasteries of this realm wherein, thanks be to God,
35 religion is right well kept and observed, be destitute of such full numbers of religious persons as they ought and may keep, hath thought good that a plain declaration should be made of the premises as well to the Lords spiritual and temporal as to other his loving subjects the Commons in this present Parliament assembled; whereupon the said Lords and Commons
40 by a great deliberation finally be resolved that it is and shall be much more to the pleasure of Almighty God and for the honour of this His realm that the possessions of such spiritual religious houses, now being spent, spoiled and wasted for increase and maintenance of sin, should be used and converted to better uses, and the unthrifty religious persons so spending
45 the same be compelled to reform their lives; And thereupon most humbly desire the King's Highness that it may be enacted by authority of this present parliament that his Majesty shall have and enjoy to him and to his heirs for ever all and singular such monasteries, priories and other religious houses of monks, canons and nuns of what kinds or diversities of
50 habits, rules or orders so ever they be called or named, which have not in lands and tenements rents tithes portions and other hereditaments above the clearly yearly value of two hundred pounds . . . .

27 Hen. VIII, c. 28: *Statutes of the Realm*, iii, 575

Questions

a How does the preamble define 'little and small abbeys, priories and other religious houses' (lines 6– 7)? What then would be the definition of a 'great and solemn monastery'?

b On what evidence ('having knowledge that the premises be true') is the case against the small monasteries stated to be based?

c 'When it came to the point it was the information contained in the *Valor Ecclesiasticus* and not the reports of the Visitors which determined the fate of each community.' Explain and comment on the likely fate under the terms of the 1536 Act of (i) an abbey with more than twelve inhabitants worth less than £200 a year, accused of 'vicious and carnal living' (ii) an abbey with less than twelve inhabitants worth more than £200 a year, accused of 'vicious and carnal living' (iii) an abbey with more than twelve inhabitants worth more than £200 a year, accused of 'vicious and carnal living'.

d Is there any evidence in the preamble to support the view that if Henry VIII's government had rested content with the partial dissolution it achieved in 1536– 7, Henry VIII would have gone down in history as an 'astute and humane reformer'?

* *e* What reasons have been put forward by modern historians for the dissolution of certain monasteries in 1536?

4 The Work of the Suppression Commissioners 1536

No community was to be dispersed under the 1536 act, unless it was a question of voluntary surrender, until the property of the house had been surveyed again and certain other information obtained. Commissioners were appointed on 24 April 1536, the same day on which the new Court of Augmentations was established specifically for the purpose of supervising the transfer to the crown of the properties and possessions of the dissolved religious houses and administering them thereafter. The commissioners for each area were made up of the appropriate regional receiver and auditor of the Court of Augmentations plus one of the clerks who had been employed in the compilation of the relevant part of the *Valor Ecclesiasticus* and three local gentlemen. Instructions were issued concerning the procedure to be followed and the kind of additional information to be obtained. When these inquiries were completed (the inquiry ended in Hertfordshire in the spring of 1537) a 'brief certificate' was sent to the Court of Augmentations where the final decisions concerning dissolution, or exemption were made. Following a decision to dissolve, the commissioners returned to organise the dispersal of the religious, make initial arrangements for the leasing of buildings and land, and the removal and sale of property and livestock. In most areas the work of dissolution proceeded smoothly, but in the autumn of 1536 the process was halted by the outbreak of the Lincolnshire rebellion and the Pilgrimage of Grace.

Extract from the Returns of the King's Commissioners for the County of Sussex, 1536

COUNTY OF SUSSEX: The brief certificate of the Commissioners appointed for the survey of the monasteries and priories within the County of Sussex as hereafter shall appear

The priory of Tortington: Black Canons of the order
5   of St. Augustine.

The clear yearly value at the first survey,	£75.	12s.	3½d.
The clear yearly value of the same house at this new survey	£82.	9s.	4½d.

with £6.17s. of increase, viz the demesnes 40s.
10 Religious persons, 6; whereof priests, 5, novices, 1,
    Incontinent, 1, desiring capacities, 4, and the others
    desire to go to other houses;
    Servants, 12; whereof waiting servants, 2; hinds, 8;
    women servants, 2; and a prior quondam having a
15   pension by resignation of £10.
Bells, lead (nil) and other buildings to be sold, by
    estimation,   £20
The house wholly in ruin.
The entire value of the movable goods, £39.5s.2d; in
20   store with farmers, nil; debts owing to the said

house £13.3s.6½d, woods there, 60 ac., all above
20 years' age, at 13s.4d. the acre, £40.
Common, 80 acres, Parks, none.
Debts owing (by the monastery)   £12. 16s.   8d.

> Public Record Office, Suppression Papers(SP5), 3/128, Cal-
> endared in *Letters and Papers, Henry VIII,* XI, p 591

Questions

a What sort of information is contained in the 'brief certificate' which is
not to be found in the *Valor Ecclesiasticus* (extract 1)?

b Suggest reasons for the discrepancy between the 'yearly value' as
revealed by the first survey (*Valor Ecclesiasticus*) and the 'new' survey
(lines 6–8).

* *c* What was the importance of the new Court of Augmentations?

5   The Final Dissolution 1537–40

In the last weeks of 1537 the first indications of a change in government
policy towards the monasteries became apparent. Until now there had
been no indication on the part of the government of any advance beyond
the policy of partial dissolution begun in 1536. There were still over 500
5 religious houses of various kinds. It is not possible to say for certain when
a decision to dissolve the remaining houses was taken, or if such a decision
was consciously taken at all. But in late 1537 and early 1538 there began
to appear signs which strongly suggest that total dissolution was by then
the ultimate aim.
10   Firstly in November 1537 the process of dissolution began again.
There were to be no further acts of suppression (the act of 1539, 31 Henry
VIII, c. 13, sometimes called the second dissolution act did not in fact
transfer to the crown any monastic property). This time the process was
carried out by 'voluntary' or 'induced' surrenders – a precedent set
15 already in the spring of 1537 with the 'voluntary' surrender of Furness
Abbey[1] – and now almost all the greater abbeys were eventually to come
into the hands of the crown as a consequence of similar acts of surrender.
     On 11 November the precedent set at Furness was repeated at Lewes in
Sussex and so began the long series of surrenders which continued almost
20 without interruption right through 1538, 1539, and the early months of
1540, ending with the surrender of Waltham Abbey on 23 March 1540.
The religious orders in England and Wales were at last extinct – for
alongside the suppression of the larger abbeys there also took place
between 1538–40 the suppression of the 180 or so houses of the
25 mendicant friars up and down the land.

1   This arose out of the abbey's suspected sympathy with the Pilgrimage of Grace.

(a) *The Surrender of the Abbot and Monks of Biddlesden* 1538

Forasmuch as we, Richard Grene, abbot of the Monastery of our Blessed
Lady Saint Mary of Biddlesden, and the convent of the same monastery
do profoundly consider that the manner and trade of living which we and
other of our pretensed religions have practised and used many days doth
5 most principally consist in certain dumb ceremonies and in certain
constitutions of Rome and other forinsecal potentates, as the abbot of
Citeaux and other in only no solid and not taught in the true knowledge
of God's laws, procuring always principally to forinsecal potentates and
powers which never came here to reform such discord of living and
10 abuses as now have been found to have reigned among us, and therefore,
now assuredly knowing that the most perfect way of living is most
principally and sufficiently declared unto us by our master, Christ, his
evangelists and apostles, and that is most expedient for us to be governed
and ordered by our own Supreme Head under God, the King's most
15 noble grace, with our mutual assent and consent do most humbly submit
ourself and every one of us unto the most benign mercy of the King's
Majesty, and by these presents do surrender and yield up unto his most
gracious hands all our said monastery, with all the lands spiritual and
temporal, tithes, rents, reversions, rights and revenues we have in all and
20 every part of the same, most humbly beseeching his Grace so to dispose of
us and of the same as shall seem best unto his most gracious pleasure.

And further in like humble manner desiring his most noble Grace to
grant unto every one of us under his letters patent some annuity or other
manner of living whereby we may be assured to have our sustenance in
25 time coming.

And further to grant unto us freely his licence to change our habits into
secular fashion, and to receive such manner of living as other secular
priests be wont to have, and all we and every one of us shall faithfully pray
unto Almighty God long to preserve his Grace with increase of much
30 felicity.

In witness whereof we have subscribed our names and put our convent
seal into these presents the 25 day of September in the thirtieth year of the
reign of our sovereign lord King Henry the Eighth.

Rymer, *Foedera*, xiv, p 610

(b) *The Surrender of the Grey Friars of Bedford*

Forasmuch as we, the Warden and friars of the house of St. Francis in
Bedford . . . do profoundly consider that the perfection of Christian
living doth not consist in dumb ceremonies, wearing of a grey coat,
disguising ourselves after strange fashions, ducking and becking, in
5 girding ourselves with a girdle full of knots, and other like papistical
ceremonies, wherein we have been most principally practised and misled
in times past . . . being minded hereafter to conform our self unto the
will and pleasure of our Supreme Head under God in earth . . . do
surrender . . . .

Rymer, *Foedera*, xiv, p 611

Questions

a   What evidence is there in these two documents of an apparent desire
    on the part of the religious to be released from a life of 'idleness and
    superstition'? Contrast the preambles to these deeds of surrender
    with the preamble to the act of 1536 (extract 3).

b   Is there any evidence in 5(a) that total abolition was now the ultimate
    intention of the government? (Refer again to extract 3.)

c   There are certain similarities of wording in extracts 5(a) and 5(b):
    what would this suggest?

* d   Suggest reasons why the friaries were not dissolved until 1538–40.

* e   What was the significance of the statute of 1539 'which has often been
    mistakenly regarded as a second act authorising the dissolution of
    monasteries'?

6   The Disposal of Monastic Lands

. . . Until late in the nineteenth century historians commonly believed
that there was little to be said about the disposal of the monastic lands. It
was considered a sin or a crime on the part of Henry VIII and those who
had benefited at the expense of the church. 'Spoliation', 'pillage' and
5   'sacrilege' were the words most frequently used in discussing the matter;
it was deemed self-evident that the nobility and gentry close to the court
had received handsome bargains in land through Henry's largesse and
that as far as the nation at large was concerned little benefit had
resulted . . . .
10   As long as historians and antiquarians drew their inspiration from
established oral traditions about the fate of the lands, from a few easily
accessible documents and, particularly from ruined monastic sites, no
different interpretation was possible . . . But a sweeping mistake had
been based on what later turned out to be only a small part of the
15 evidence.
      More recent approaches to the subject reflect the growing sophisti-
cation of historical method at large: the quest for further source materials;
the analysis of old sources in new ways; the attempt to apply techniques
from other disciplines (such as mathematics and statistics); the regular
20 reshaping of historical consensus on the issues raised and a developing
awareness of their complexity.
      Our field of study may instructively be compared with an archae-
ological site. For generations men were satisfied with established tradition
as to its nature and content and a few pieces of evidence found near the
25 surface were enough to confirm their beliefs. But in the past century or so
successive specialists have cut cross-sections through parts of the site, from
differing angles, and reported their findings. Each in turn felt that his own
cross-section might hold the clue to the real nature of the site as a whole,
only to discover later that the next man's findings in some respects

30 modified or contradicted his own. This model is also valid in other
respects: for instance, some of the evidence no longer survives and some
of it is buried so deep that it may never be unearthed. The final report has
yet to be written but we already have a formidable amount of analysis
before us to warn that there is no simple answer to most of the questions
35 we should like to ask and that we can only begin to understand the whole
'site' by noting the angles and limits of some of the cross-sections . . . .
    Only towards the end of the nineteenth century did historians really
become aware of the wealth of surviving evidence on the disposal of the
monastic lands. . . . There was now too much material . . . for any one
40 scholar to master, producing a definitive monograph on the monastic
lands which would not be overtaken by subsequent research. But a start
had to be made somewhere . . . .
    A. Savine of Moscow University produced a masterly study of *Valor
Ecclesiasticus* (1909) and went on to study the letters patent by which the
45 Crown granted away many of the lands. His research at once demonstrated that the accepted tradition was wrong: much of the land had
been *sold* by Henry VIII or exchanged for other plots then in private
hands. Much less had been given away than earlier scholars had assumed.
Other writers have gone on to show that good (i.e. market) prices were
50 paid for most of the lands sold; that sales began in earnest after
Cromwell's fall and accelerated from 1543 as warfare made increasing
inroads into revenue . . . .
    Given this new understanding of the evidence, it was clear that scholars
had to work on selected regions, attempting to assimilate every layer of
55 evidence, rather than hope to cover the whole country. . . . But . . .
considerable regional variations in the findings. . . . make it dangerous to
rely too heavily on figures produced for any one area. A vertical
specialisation (by area) . . . has almost as many pitfalls as a horizontal one
(by type of document). Yet without such studies we should never get any
60 nearer to our final report on the impact of the dissolution on English
society.
    Historians are now agreed that most of the land disposed of by Henry
VIII went to persons already well placed in the social or governmental
hierarchy. Most of the nobility . . . acquired lands by gift, exchange or
65 purchase. But the majority of sales were made to gentry, courtiers, crown
officials, lawyers and townsmen, many of whom already had strong local
connections. . . . It is likely that men who already had the spending
power would soon have deployed their assets in some similar investment
even without the dissolution which, however, must have speeded up the
70 process . . . . For some, receipt of the land was the clinching factor
which raised their social status . . . . But for others, similar purchases in
the private land market could equally well achieve the same result . . . .
    In an important local study J. E. Kew has recently shown that, at least in
Devon, there were more dealings in the private land market, in terms of
75 both the numbers of transactions and the amount of land changing hands,
than in the crown land market following the dissolution. If this was so

over the whole country it would further minimise the special role of the
dissolution in affecting the social balance. Kew's work shows that we may
not view the dissolution in isolation from other economic and social
80   developments. Returning to our archaeological analogy, there might
well be important evidence over the hedge in an adjacent site! . . .
   Historians discussing the rise of the gentry or the 'crisis of the
aristocracy' have differed widely in their interpretation of factors
affecting mobility within and between classes and even in identifying the
85   component parts of a given class. But it is generally agreed that such
processes can only be safely studied over a long time-scale, taking as
many individual examples into account as possible . . . . Few studies in
the disposal of monastic lands have continued beyond the year
1558 . . . . The long term effects of the dissolution have, therefore, not
90   been systematically explored. . . . The full impact of the dissolution on
English government and administration cannot be ascertained from
studies confined to the reign of Henry VIII, nor can the impact on English
society be fully understood without taking into account later sales and the
leases by which so much of the property was held until well after the reign
95   of Henry VIII. Only recently have scholars begun to extend their horizons
in these directions and little of their work has yet been published. . . .
   But the general conclusion which may be drawn...so far is that we
must not be misled into thinking that small samples of the surviving
evidence are necessarily typical of the whole. More studies, local and
100   central, are still needed. More evidence is still to be quarried and there
may be valuable clues also in neighbouring fields. Above all, we must not
select too short a time-scale for our studies.
   Christopher Kitching, 'The Disposal of Monastic and Chantry
   Lands', in *Church and Society in England: Henry VIII to James I*, eds
   Heal and O'Day, 1977, pp 119–28

Questions

a   What views about the disposal of monastic lands were held 'until late
    in the nineteenth century' (line 1)? What criticisms could now be
    made of those views?
b   Comment on Kitching's examples of 'the growing sophistication of
    historical method' (lines 16–21).
c   Summarise the present state of knowledge about the disposal of
    monastic lands and the impact on English society.
d   How does this topic illustrate the advantages and the disadvantages of
    the study of local history?
* e   Will it ever be possible to write a 'definitive monograph' (line 40) or a
       'final report' (line 32) on this – or any other – topic?

V The Mid-Tudor Crisis
(i) 1547—53

Introduction

On 27 January 1547, King Henry VIII, the 'Stalin of Tudor England',[1] died and left to a sickly nine year old boy the crown and an 'evil inheritance'.[2] Henry bequeathed a heavy debt, a debased coinage, a shaken administrative system, an unsettled doctrine and a nation divided in religion. There was an uneasy truce with France and a war with Scotland. Within three days of Henry's death, Edward Seymour became protector of the realm, after a *coup*, engineered by himself. This raised the possibility of a factional struggle, complicated and intensified by religion, taking place against a background of acute social and economic problems.

The whole economy appeared to be upset. 'Greedy cormorants (have) enclosed from the poor their due commons (and) levied greater fines than heretofore. . . . ' Rents were increasing. Manufactures seemed to be declining and exports falling. Prices were high and rising, as was unemployment, and wages were inadequate. In the countryside there was universal discontent; though, arguably, the economic problems were being felt even more keenly in the towns and boroughs of the land, compounding the urban decay which had developed since the 1520s.[3]

'Scarcytie, famyn, sickenes be plages of god', sent upon the people for their wickedness, wrote John Hales, about 1549, the year which saw the first of three consecutive bad harvests, the first English Prayer Book, and risings in Somerset, Wiltshire, Hampshire, Kent, Sussex, Essex, Devon, Cornwall, Northamptonshire, Bedfordshire, Buckinghamshire, Oxfordshire, Yorkshire, East Anglia, Leicestershire and Rutland.[4] The 'English sweat', absent since 1529, made an unwelcome return in 1551. A second, revolutionary, Prayer Book in 1552 was followed by the death of the 'boy tyrant'[5] in 1553.

To contemporary writers the religious question, not always divorced from social and economic problems, was paramount. Some recent historians writing on the mid-sixteenth century have seen a unity in the era the keynote of which was 'crisis', but Professor Elton has warned, 'The question remains whether difficulties really run deep enough to enable us to speak of a crisis at all. True the notion has got established among historians . . . (but) we are in danger of accepting yet another Tudor orthodoxy too trustingly.'[6]

1   W. G. Hoskins, *Age of Plunder* (1976) p 232
2   G. R. Elton, *England under the Tudors* (1974) p 202
3   W. R. D. Jones, *The Mid-Tudor Crisis 1539–1563* (1973) chapter 5; R. Tittler, 'The Incorporation of Boroughs 1540–1558', *History*, 62 (1977) p 35
4   M. L. Bush, *The Government Policy of Protector Somerset* (1975) p 34
5   G. R. Elton, *Reform and Reformation* (1977) p 372
6   G. R. Elton, *History*, 60 (1975) p 116, reviewing W. R. D. Jones, op. cit.

Further Reading

The most recent synthesis of work on this period is G. R. Elton, *Reform and Reformation* (1977). M. L. Bush, *The Government Policy of Protector Somerset* (1975) and D. E. Hoak, *The King's Council in the Reign of Edward vi* (1976) have demolished much of the traditional story of Edward vi's reign. A. G. Dickens, *The English Reformation* (1972) is essential for an understanding of the religious changes in this period. Anthony Fletcher, *Tudor Rebellions* (1968) analyses the demands of the rebels in 1549. Julian Cornwall, *Revolt of the Peasantry* (1977) considers the risings in the South West and East Anglia as military operations. See also Jeremy Goring, 'Social Change and Military Decline in Mid-Tudor England', *History*, 60 (1975). Stephen Land has taken a fresh look at *Kett's Rebellion* (1977), which supplements the classic study by S. T. Bindoff (1949). Peter Ramsey, *Tudor Economic Problems* (1963) is a useful introduction.

1   Religious Changes during Edward vi's Reign 1547–8 and 1550

Item the v day after in September [1547] beganne the kynges vysytation at Powlles, and alle images pulled down; . . . and so all imagys pullyd downe thorrow alle Ynglonde att that tyme, and all churches new whytte-lymed, with the commandmenttes wryttne on the walles . . . .

5   *Item* the xvii day of the same monythe [November] at nyghte was pullyd downe the Rode in Powlles with Mary and John, with all the images ofe the churche . . . .

Item also at that same time was pullyd down thorrow alle the kynges domynyon in every churche alle Roddes with alle images. . . . Also this

10   same tyme was moche spekyng agayne the sacrament of the auter, that some called it Jacke of the boxe, with divers other shamefulle names; and then was made a proclamacyon agayne it, and so contynewyd; and at Ester followyng there began the commonion and confession but of thoys that wolde, as the boke doth specifythe. And at this tyme was moche

15   prechyng agayne the masse. And the sacrament of the auter pullyd downe in dyvers places thorrow the realme . . . .

Item after Ester began the servis in Ynglyshe at Powles and also in dyvers other pariche churches . . . .

Item also this yere was Barking chappylle pulled down . . . and also

20   Strand churche to make the protector duke of Somerset's place larger.

Item this yere was alle the chaunterys put downe . . . .

Item on Trenyte sonday [1550] preched doctor Kyrkame, and sayd that in
the sacrament was no substance but brede and wynne.

Item on sente Barnabes day was kepte no holiday through alle London at
25 the commandement of the mayor, and at nyght was the aulter in Powlles
pullyd downe, and as that day the vayelle was hongyd up benethe the
steppes and the tabulle sett up there; and as sennet after there the
comunion was mynystered . . . .

Item the last day of August preched at the crosse Stephin Caston, and there
30 spake agayne the lady Mary asmoche as he myghte, but he namyd not
hare, but sayd there was a gret woman within the realme that was a gret
supporter and mayntayner of popery and superstycione. . . . And also he
sayd that kyne Henry the viijth was a papyst, with many obprobryus
wordes of hym as yt was harde.

> *Chronicle of the Grey Friars of London*, ed. J. G. Nichols, Camden
> Society, 1852, pp 54–6, 67

Questions

a What evidence is there in this extract of changes in (i) ritual (ii)
doctrine, in the first twenty months of the reign of Edward VI?

b What *internal* evidence is there to establish the dating of this
document?

* c 'Item this yere was alle the chaunterys put downe' (line 21). What
were the causes and the consequences of the Edwardian dissolution?

d Comment on the references to (i) 'Henry the viijth' (line 33) (ii) 'the
protector duke of Somerset' (line 20) (iii) 'the lady Mary' (line 30).

e Of what value to the historian is the authorship and date of this
document?

2 The Prayer Books of Edward VI

(a) The First Prayer Book 1549: extracts from the Communion Service

*The Priest standing humbly afore the middes of the Altar, shall saie the Lordes
praier* . . . . *Then shall the Prieste first receive the Communion in both kindes
himselfe, and next deliver it to other Ministers, if any there be present . . . and
after to the people.*

5 *And when he delivereth the Sacramente of the body of Christe, he shall say to
every one these wordes.*

The body of our Lorde Jesus Christe whiche was geven for thee, preserve
thy bodye and soule unto everlasting lyfe.

*And the Minister delivering the Sacramente of the bloud, and geving every one to
10 drinke once and no more, shall say,*

The bloud of our Lorde Jesus Christe which was shed for thee, preserve
thy bodye and soule unto everlastyng lyfe.

(b) The Second Prayer Book 1552: extracts from the Communion Service

The Table havyng at the Communion tyme a fayre whyte lynen clothe upon it
shall stande in the body of the Churche, or in the chauncell . . . And the Priest
standing at the north syde of the Table, shall saye the Lordes prayer . . . .
. . . Then the Priest standing up shal saye, as foloweth. . . . Heare us O
5 mercyefull father wee beseeche thee; and graunt that wee, receyving
these they creatures of bread and wyne, according to thy sonne our
Savioure Jesus Christ's holy institucion, in remembraunce of his death
and passion, may be partakers of his most blessed body and bloud; who, in
the same night that he was betrayed, tooke bread, and when he had geven
10 thanks, he brake it, and gave it to his Disciples, sayinge: Take, eate, this is
my bodye which is geven for you. Doe this in remembraunce of me.
Lykewyse after supper he tooke the cup, and when he had geven thankes,
he gave it to them, sayinge: Drink ye all of this, for this is my bloud of the
new Testament whiche is shed for you and for many, for remission of
15 synnes; do this as oft as ye shall drinke it in remembraunce of me.
Then shall the minister first receyve the Communion in both kyndes
hymselfe . . . and after the people in their handes kneling Take and eate this, in
remembraunce that Christ dyed for thee, and feede on him in thy hearte
by faythe, with thanksgeving.
20 Drinke this in remembraunce that Christe's bloude was shed for thee, and
be thankefull.

(c) The 'Black Rubric' 1552

. . . Whereas it is ordeyned in the boke of Common Prayer, in the
administracion of the Lord's Supper, that the Communicants kneling
shoulde receyve the holye Communion: . . . leste the same kneelyng
myght be thought or taken otherwyse, we dooe declare that it is not ment
5 thereby, that any adoracion is doone . . . either unto the Sacramentall
bread or wyne there bodily receyved, or unto anye reall and essenciall
presence there beeyng of Christe's naturall fleshe and bloude. For as
concernynge the Sacramentall bread and wynne, they remayne still in
theyr verye naturall sybstaunces, and therefore may not be adored, for
10 that were Idolatrye. . . . And as concernynge the naturall body and
bloud of our saviour Christ they are in heaven and not here. For it is
agaynst the trueth of Christes true natural bodye, to be in more places
than in one, at one tyme.

Questions

a What evidence is there in extract (a) of (i) change (ii) continuity (iii)
compromise?

* *b* 'Except in the West, the Prayer Book of 1549 appears to have been
quietly though not enthusiastically received.' How would you
explain this acceptance?

c 'Drastic changes were introduced in 1552 – changes which are most marked in the Communion Service.' Compare and contrast extracts (a) and (b).

d Explain the inclusion in the Prayer Book of 1552 of the so-called 'Black Rubric', extract (c).

* *e* To what extent was England in 1553 a protestant realm?

3 (a) The Demands of the Western Rebels 1549

2 Item we will have the lawes of our soverayne lord king Henry the viii concernynge the syxe articles, to be in use agayn, as in hys time they were.

3 Item we will have the masse in latten, as was before, and celebrated by the Pryest wythoute any man or woman communycating wyth hym.

5 4 Item we wyll have the Sacrament hange over the hyeghe aulter, and there by worshypped as it was wount to be, and they whiche will not thereto consent, we wyl have them dye lyke heretykes . . . .

5 Item we wyll have the Sacrament of the aulter but at Easter delyvered to the lay people and then but in one kynde . . . .

10 7 Item . . . Images to be set up again in every church and all other auncient olde Ceremonyes used heretofore, by our mother the holy church.

8 Item we will not receyve the newe service because it is but lyke a Christmas game, but we will have oure olde service of Mattens, masse,

15 Evensong and procession in Latten not in English, as it was before. And so we the Cornyshe men (whereof certen of us understande no Englysh) utterly refuse thys new Englysh.

9 Item we wyll have everye preacher in his sermon, and every Pryest at hys masse, praye specially by name for the soules in purgatory, as oure

20 forefathers dyd.

10 Item we wyll have the whole Byble and al bokes of scripture in Englysh to be called in agayn, for we be enformed that otherwise the clergye, shal not of long time confound the heretykes . . . .

13 Item we wyll that no Gentleman shall have anye mo servantes then

25 one to wayte upo hym excepte he maye dispend one hundreth marke land and for every hundreth marke we thynke it reasonable, he should have a man and no mo.

14 Item we wyll that the halfe parte of the abbey landes and Chauntrye landes, in everye mans possessyons how so ever he cam by them, be geven

30 again to two places, where two of the chief Abbeis was with in every Countye, where suche half part shalbe taken out, and there to be establyshed a place for devout persons, whych shall pray for the Kyng and the common wealth, and to the same we wyll have al the almes of the Churche box geven for these seven yeres, and for thys article we desire

35 that we may name half of the Commissioners . . . .[1]

F. Rose-Troup, *The Western Rebellion of 1549*, 1913, pp 220–3

1 There were a total sixteen articles in the final manifesto drawn up outside Exeter.

Questions

* a When and where did the so-called 'Prayer Book Rebellion' take place?

  b How true is it that the demands of the western rebels amounted to 'a manifesto for a return to catholicism'?

  c 'To interpret the rebellion as solely religious would be an over-simplification.' Comment.

  d Did the risings in the west and in the east (extract 3(b)) have anything in common?

* e 'More widespread rioting and rebellion occurred in 1549 than in any other year in the Tudor century.' How would you account for this?

(b) 'Ket's Demands being in Rebellion' 1549

1 We pray your grace that where it is enacted for inclosyng that it be not hurtfull to suche as have enclosed saffren grounds for they be gretly chargeablye to them, and that from hensforth noman shall enclose any more . . . .

5 3 We pray your grace that no lord of mannor shall comon upon the Comons.

4 We pray that prests from hensforth shall purchase no lands neyther ffre nor Bondy, and the lands that they have in possession may be letten to temporall men, as they wer in the fyrst yere of the reign of Kyng Henry
10 the vii.

5 We pray that Redeground and medowe grounde may be at such price as they were in the ffirst yere of King Henry the vii . . . .

8 We pray that priests or vicars that be not able to preche and sett forthe the woorde of god to hys parisheners may be thereby putt from his
15 benefyce, and the parisheners there to chose an other or else the pateron or lord of the towne . . . .

11 We pray that all ffreholders and copieholders may take the profights of all comons and then to comon, and the lords not to comon nor take profights of the same . . . .

20 14 We pray that copiehould land that is onreasonable rented may go as it dyd in the first yere of King henry vii and that at the deth of a tenante or of a sale the same lands to be charged with an easy ffyne as a capon or a reasonable some of money for a remembraunce.

15 We pray that no prest shall be a chaplain nor no other officer to eny
25 man of honour of wyrshypp but only to be resydent uppon ther benefices whereby ther parysheners may be entrusted with the lawes of God.

16 We pray that alle bonde men may be made ffre for god made all ffre with his precious blode sheddyng . . . .

20 We pray that evry propriatoril parson or vicar havyng a benefice of
30 £10 or more by yere shall eyther by themselves or by some other

persone teche pore mens chyldren of ther paryshe the boke called the
cathakysme and the prymer . . . .

21 We pray that it be not lawfull to the lords of eny manner to purchase
lands frely and to lett them out ageyn by copie of court roll [according to
35 the custom of the manor] to ther gret advauncement and to the undoyng
of your pore subjects . . . .

22 We pray that no propriatoril parson or vicar in consideracion of
avoyding Trobyll and sute between them and ther pore parishners
whiche they daly do procede and attempt shall from hensforth take for the
40 full contentacon of all the tenthes which now they do receyve but viiid. of
the noble [a flat rate of 10 per cent] in the full discharge of all other
tythes.

26 We pray that no lord knyght nor gentlemaᶇ shall have or take in
ferme any spirituall promocion . . . .

45 29 We pray that no lorde knyght esquyer nor gentleman do graze nor
fede eny bullocks or shepe if he may spende forty pounds a yere by his
lands but only for the provicion of his howse. [1]

> By me Robert Ket
> By me Thomas Aldryche
> Thomas Cod (Mayor of Norwich)

F. W. Russell, *Ket's Rebellion in Norfolk*, 1859, pp 48 – 56.

1   There are a total of twenty-nine articles. Thirteen deal specifically with 'agricultural'
problems; seven (all included above) may be classified as 'anti-clerical'.

Questions

* *a* When and where did Ket's rebellion take place? To whom are the
'Demands' addressed, and why?

b 'Not a revolt against the protestant government but against the
Norfolk gentry.' Enumerate and explain the grievances against local
landlords set out above.

c What evidence is there in the articles of the extent to which the rebels
were motivated by 'religion'?

d Comment on article 16 (lines 27 – 8).

* *e* What were the reasons for the eventual failure of Ket's rebellion?

* *f* Could either of the main risings of 1549 have succeeded?

4 Dearth – in the Midst of Plenty

Husbandman Marry for these inclosures do undo us all, for they make us
pay dearer for our land that we occupy . . . all is taken up for pastures,
either for sheep or for grazing of cattle. . . . By these inclosures men
do lack livings and be idle. . . . Moreover all things are so dear that by
5 their daily labour they are not able to live.

Capper I have well experience thereof, for I am fain to give my

journeymen 2d. a day more than I was wont to, and yet they say they
cannot sufficiently live thereon. And I know for a truth that the best
husband of them all can save but little at the year's end; and by reason of
10 such dearth as ye speak of, we that are artificers can keep few or no
apprentices like as we were wont to do . . . .

Merchant ˙ So the most part of all the towns of England, London
excepted . . . are decayed sore in their houses, streets and other
buildings . . . also the country in their highways and bridges; for such
15 poverty reigneth everywhere that few men have so much to spare as they
may give anything to (their) reparation . . . . There is such a general
dearth of all things as I never knew the like, not only of things growing
within this realm, but also of all other merchandise that we buy beyond
the seas. . . . I wot well all these do cost me more by the third part well,
20 than they did but seven years ago. Then all kind of victual are as dear or
dearer again, and no cause of God's part thereof, as far as I can perceive:
for I never saw more plenty of corn, grass and cattle of all sort than we
have at this present, and have had these three years past continually . . . .

Knight Since ye have plenty of corn and cattle as ye say, then it should
25 seem this dearth should be long of [should not be attributed to] these
inclosures; for it is not by scarceness of corn that we have this dearth, for
thanks be to God corn is good cheap . . . yet I confess there is a
wonderful dearth of all things; and that do I, and all men of my sort, feel
most grief in, which have no wares to sell, or occupation to live by, but
30 only our lands. . . . You may and do raise the price of your wares as the
price of victuals and other necessaries do rise. . . . We cannot do so of our
lands, that is already in the hands of other men. . . . In all my lifetime I
look not that the third part of my land shall come to my disposition, that I
may enhance the rent of the same . . . .

35 *Doctor* And now I must come to that thing which I take to be the chief
cause of all this dearth of things, and of the manifest impoverishment of
this realm . . . that is the basing or rather corrupting of our coin and
treasure . . . .

Sir Thomas Smith, *A Discourse of the Common Weal of this Realm of
England* (1549?)

Questions

a   What evidence of inflation is to be found in these extracts?
b   What evidence is there of general economic dislocation?
c   Compare the views of the Husbandman and the Knight about
    enclosures, prices and rents.
d   Comment on the paradox noted by the Merchant: that food prices
    were high when there was no shortage of food.
e   Comment on the view expressed by Dr Pandotheus.

5 The 'Good Duke': Edward Seymour, Earl of Hertford and Duke of Somerset, Lord Protector

(a) The traditional view

'This strange and complex man . . . was one of the architects of the modern world'; but he 'displayed an almost incredible want of administrative sensitivity in trying to push through a (social) policy which lacked the essential approval and cooperation of the governing
5 classes and he justified their worst forebodings by exciting illegal action in those it was designed to help'. Because Protector Somerset sympathised with the rebels of 1549 he was reluctant to conduct effective military campaigns against them. 'The Protector's fall was followed by the complete reversal of his schemes', and the introduction of a reactionary
10 policy in place of his doctrinaire idealism.

A. F. Pollard, W. K. Jordan, *et al.*

(b) A re-interpretation

Somerset had serious differences with his colleagues on the council which eventually culminated in his fall from power. Yet these differences were not the result of an ideological conflict but of disputes over the details of policy and reactions against the personal obnoxiousness of the protector.
5 While Somerset dominated policy, he did so because his views largely coincided with his colleagues. Thus, although much of the direction and dynamism stemmed from him, the responsibility can be said to have lain with a governing group which shared a common attitude . . . .

Somerset's social concern was basically political and personal. In this
10 respect his consideration for poverty cannot be described as a genuine concern for the plight of the poor. Poverty was appreciated as a cause of military insufficiency and peasant insurrection, and as a means of earning virtue by remedial acts of justice and charity. . . . Somerset had some concern for the lower orders but because he subscribed to common
15 aristocratic feelings, not because of an unusual compassion. As a ruler he acted conventionally for the preservation of the state; as a person he sought for a virtuous reputation. . . . Somerset succeeded only to the extent of acquiring a reputation for goodness in spite of his activities as a builder of sumptuous houses, as a sheep master, as an encloser and a rack-
20 renter; but by the time of his fall even his reputation was not what he would have wished, having become entangled with a reputation for radicalism, largely because of his behaviour towards peasant rebels . . . .

Persistent peasant risings were a particular problem to Somerset in 1549 because they endangered his top-priority project . . . in Scotland.
25 The government could not afford to confront the Scots and peasant rebels with armies simultaneously. It therefore faced a problematical choice of . . . allowing Scottish affairs to degenerate even further, or of risking domestic chaos through delaying military action against the rebels. The war with France which finally broke out on 8 August presented a further
30 problem. At this stage, having postponed the Scottish project in order to

deal with the rebels, Somerset now came under pressure to put his house in order to confront the French. The risings acquired a critical importance because they occurred in a time of political crisis when the government was without funds and at war abroad on two fronts.

35 Because of the state's traditional deficiencies and his present foreign commitments, Somerset had difficulty in taking action against the rebels, but not in deciding to oppose them. He doubtlessly sympathised with their economic grievances . . . But Somerset did not favour rebellion. . . . His attitude towards rebellion was thoroughly critical and
40 conventional. Rebels were 'lewd, seditious and evil disposed persons'. . . . No matter what was said at Somerset's trial, the government's treatment of rebellion in 1549 was not hindered by an unusual sympathy for it, a fact emphatically demonstrated by Somerset's extensive surviving correspondence on the subject.

45 Partly responsible for the government's initial attitude towards the summer risings of 1549 was its earlier success in quelling the spring risings without the use of force. . . . By winkling out the ringleaders, hearing grievances, promising remedy and offering a pardon for the rebels who returned home, the risings were pacified unobtrusively and economically
50 and without the mobilisation of troops. ，. . This initial success heavily influenced the government's approach to the summer risings. It proceeded against the first of them, the western rising, in a similarly discreet and indirect manner. . . . 'We would ye were . . . quietly pacified than rigorously persecuted'. . . . From first to last the government's main aim
55 was to end the western rising in the quietest and most economical manner possible. . . . When the offers of pardon and promises of remedy failed to bring results, it resorted without compunction to military force. A similar procedure was followed in East Anglia. . . . Running through the government's policy towards the risings as a whole was a thread of
60 consistency which rendered the treatment of the East Anglians and the westerners remarkably alike. The differences certainly cannot be seen as a victory of a hard-line policy over one of gentleness which replaced Somerset by Warwick as leader of the force directed against Ket. Warwick's leadership produced no radical change in the approach to
65 peasant rebellion. . . . In view of the consistency of a policy which seemed a response to practical considerations not radical ideas, and also considering the fact that the government's instructions on rebellion usually took the form of conciliar dispatches . . . the government's response to the summer risings seems to have rested on a consensus of
70 opinion in the council and on shifting circumstances rather than upon the idealism of one man who in the later stages of the risings happened to be overborne.

In quelling disorder, the government's policy towards the rebellions of 1549 was eminently successful. . . . Somerset's effective, efficient and
75 flexible treatment of rebellion contrasted sharply with his disastrous Scottish programme and his ineffectual programme of social reform. Nevertheless, the aristocracy did not allow it to count in his favour. They

failed to appreciate its subtlety and practicality, and because of it they branded him a radical. He did not have this reputation before the risings.
80 It cannot be seen as a product of his programme of social reform. Men only came to see him in this light when his social programme proved to be a cause of insurrection, and when it seemed that Somerset was prepared to allow the insurrections some licence. The charge of unwarranted leniency towards the risings was made by Paget, Smith and
85 Russell, who criticised the reliance on pardons and proclamations and advocated the application of force. The next step was to explain this supposed leniency in terms of sympathy. . . . Because of the aristocracy's extreme conception of rebellion, sympathy for it implied support for revolution. The final step was, in the light of this leniency, to re-assess
90 Somerset's social programme as an attack on the traditional order. . . . By late 1549, as a result of his policy towards insurrection and the new light it seemed to throw upon his social aims, Somerset had acquired a widely accepted public reputation as a radical. . . . Because of this reputation, his overthrow was easily accomplished. There was no
95 question of Somerset deserving the reputation. . . . The policy of Edward VI's other government differed from Somerset's not only on account of Somerset's downfall but also because the war ended in 1550, the harvest failed in 1549, 1550 and 1551, and the cloth trade slumped in 1551 and 1552.

M. L. Bush, *The Government Policy of Protector Somerset*, 1975, pp 4, 57–8, 87–9, 90, 93–5, 97–8, 161

Questions

a   'It would be churlish to deny Somerset a genuine concern about social justice.' Would it, according to Dr Bush?

b   Did Somerset hesitate to take military action against the rebels in 1549 because he sympathised with them?

c   What was Somerset's policy towards the rebels?

d   Why does Dr Bush believe that government policy rested on a consensus of opinion in the Council?

*   e   What was Somerset's 'programme of social reform' (line 76)? Why did it 'prove to be a cause of insurrection' (lines 81–2)

f   How does Dr Bush explain Somerset's reputation as a radical?

VI   The Mid-Tudor Crisis
(ii) 1553—8

Introduction

If rebellion is defined as an armed rising against established government, then the support for Mary in 1553 was such a rebellion; indeed, it was the only successful rebellion in the sixteenth century. Sir Nicholas Throckmorton succinctly expressed the reasons for Mary's success:

> And though I liked not the religion
> Which all her life Queen Mary had professed,
> Yet in my mind that wicked notion
> Right heirs for to displace, I did detest.

Mary, aged thirty-seven, the first woman to occupy the throne in her own right, half-Spanish and staunchly catholic, proceeded to dissipate any fund of goodwill by marrying her cousin Philip of Spain, by embarking upon a policy of religious persecution (Professor A. G. Dickens, and others, trace the origins of this policy to the Queen herself, though this is denied by her sympathetic biographer, Miss H. F. M. Prescott), and, ultimately, by involving England in a disastrous war.

The political and religious problems of the reign must be seen against a background of prolonged economic crisis – Professor Bindoff's 'dangerous corner' in English economic and social history – the worst in living memory, in intensity and in effect. There were disastrous harvests in 1555 and in 1556, the latter being the worst between 1480 and 1620. In that year 'the scarcity of bread was so great in so much that the plain poor people did make much of acorns and drank water'; whilst 'a sickness of strong fever did molest them'. This is a reference to the influenza epidemic which, it has been estimated, from a study of wills, between 1556 and 1560, caused the death rate to average about 150 per cent above the norm.

Mary 'failed', it has been claimed, as much because she was a 'Spanish' Tudor as because she was a Roman Catholic; but there is a new attitude abroad. 'All was not failure in Mary's reign', and the keynote is no longer seen entirely as one of 'sterility'. Conrad Russell, for example, has argued that many of the difficulties of Mary's reign are seen with historical hindsight and are consequently exaggerated. Much discussion of the reign, therefore, scarcely rises above the level of *1066 And All That*. In financial and economic affairs, Russell finds evidence of 'quiet efficiency'.

If only Mary had lived another fifteen years . . . .

As it was, 'Perhaps no other reign in English history has seen such a great endeavour made, and so utterly defeated. All that Mary did was undone, all she intended utterly unfulfilled.' H. F. M. Prescott, *Mary Tudor*, 1952

Further Reading

The succession problem is dealt with in S. T. Bindoff, 'A Kingdom at Stake', *History Today*, October 1953; and M. Levine, *Tudor Dynastic Problems, 1460–1571* (1973). For the religious aspects of the reign see, in addition to A. G. Dickens, *The English Reformation* (1972), Claire Cross, *Church and People, 1450–1660* (1976); D. M. Loades, *Politics and the Nation, 1450–1660* (1974); and D. M. Loades, *The Oxford Martyrs* (1970). Both Conrad Russell, *The Crisis of Parliaments: English History 1509–1660* (1971), and C. S. L. Davies, *Peace, Print and Protestantism* (1976), see some positive achievements in Mary's reign in financial and economic affairs. W. R. D. Jones, *The Mid-Tudor Crisis, 1539–1563* (1973) denies that these had anything to do with Mary. G. R. Elton, *Reform and Reformation* (1977) believes that Mary died just in time. The most recent assessment of Mary Tudor is *Bloody Mary* by Carolly Erickson (1978).

1 Lady Jane Grey

. . . And forasmuch as . . . the said Lady Mary and Lady Elizabeth, being illegitimate and not lawfully begotten . . . whereby . . . the said Lady Mary as also the said Lady Elizabeth to all intents and purposes are and be clearly disabled to ask, claim or challenge the . . . imperial
5 crown . . . as also for that the said Lady Mary and Lady Elizabeth be unto us but of the half blood, and therefore by the ancient laws, statutes, and customs of this realm be not inheritable unto us, although they were legitimate, as they be not indeed. And forasmuch also . . . that if the said Lady Mary or Lady Elizabeth should hereafter have . . . the said imperial
10 crown of this realm, and should then happen to marry with any stranger born out of this realm, that the same would rather adhere and practice to have the laws and customs of his . . . own native country . . . to be practised or put in use within this realm, than the laws, statutes, and customs here of long time used . . . which would then tend to the utter
15 subversion of the commonwealth of this our realm. . . . UPON ALL WHICH CAUSES AND MATTERS . . . we have weighed and considered . . . what ways and means were most convenient to be had for the stay of our succession. . . . And calling to our remembrance that the Lady Jane, the Lady Catherine, and the Lady Mary, daughters of our
20 entirely beloved cousin the Lady Frances, now wife to our loving cousin and faithful counsellor, Henry, duke of Suffolk . . . being very nigh of our whole blood, of the part of our father's side, and being natural-born here within the realm, and have been also very honourably brought up

and exercised in good and godly learning and other noble virtues . . . WE
25 THEREFORE . . . do declare . . . that the said imperial crown . . . shall
for lack of issue of our body, remain, come and be unto (1) THE ELDEST
SON OF THE BODY OF THE SAID LADY FRANCES . . . (or) (2) TO THE
LADY JANE . . . and to the heirs male of the said Lady Jane . . . .

Letters Patent for the limitation of the Crown, 21 June 1553

Questions

*   a Comment on (i) the authorship (ii) the timing of this document.
    b What reasons are given for the exclusion of 'the Lady Mary' and 'the
       Lady Elizabeth' from the succession?
    c What qualifications and qualities are said to be possessed by the Grey
       line?
    d Consider carefully, the wording of the last section beginning 'WE
       THEREFORE . . .' (lines 24–25 ff). What problems is it designed to
       solve?
    e 'The letters patent presented arguments designed to give the
       appearance of right to that which never could be right.' Do you
       agree?
*   f How would you explain the failure of the attempt to put Lady Jane
       Grey on the throne?

2 Wyatt's Rebellion 1554

Note, that the xxvth of January (1554) the council was certified that there
was up in Kent Sir Thomas Wyatt (and others) . . . for the said quarrel in
resisting the said King of Spain, as they said, their pretence was this only
and none other, and partly for moving certain councillors from about the
5 queen . . . .
   The xxvith day it was noised that Rochester bridge was taken by the
rebels. . . . The same day there was made ready (in London) . . . about
five hundred of harnessed men (the Whitecoats) . . . and the Sunday
following they went towards Gravesend against the Kentish men . . . .
10   . . . And as the company was set in a readiness and marched forward
toward the bridge, Bret, being captain of the five hundred Londoners . . . turned himself about, and drawing out his swords, said,
by report, these or much like words: 'Masters, we go about to fight
against our native countrymen of England and our friends in a quarrel
15 unrightful and partly wicked, for they, considering the great and
manifold mysteries which are like to fall upon us if we shall be under the
rule of the proud Spaniards or strangers, are here assembled to make
resistance of the coming in of him or his favourers; and for that they know
right well, that if we should be under their subjection they would, as
20 slaves and villains, spoil us of our goods and lands, ravish our wives before
our faces, and deflower our daughters in our presence, have now, for the
avoiding of so great mischiefs and inconveniences likely to light not only

upon themselves but on every of us and the whole realm, have taken upon
them now, in time before his coming, this their enterprise, against which I
25 think no English heart ought to say, much less by fighting to withstand
them.' . . . The Londoners cried Awyatt! Awyatt! of which sudden noise
the duke (of Norfolk), the earl of Ormonde and the captain of the guard,
being abashed, fled forthwith . . . to London . . . which discomfiture,
like as it was . . . very displeasing to the queen and the council, even so it
30 was no less joyous to the Londoners, and most part of all others.

The Chronicle of Queen Jane and of two years of Queen Mary, ed. J.
G. Nichols, Camden Society, 1850, Vol. XLVII, pp 36–9

Questions

* *a* Who was Sir Thomas Wyatt? What is known about the extent of the
planned conspiracy of 1553–4?
   b Comment on the stated objectives of the rebels. Have any other
motives been attributed to them?
   c What evidence is there in this document that Wyatt had a real chance
of gaining the sympathy and active support of London?
   d Comment on the zenophobia revealed in this document (and in other
documents in this section).
* *e* 'Wyatt came nearer than any other Tudor rebel to toppling a
monarch from the throne.' Do you agree? Why did he fail?
* *f* With what other conspiracies was Mary faced during her reign?

3 Reconciliation with Rome

Cardinal Pole presses for an answer whether or no he is to be received here
as legate. . . . Affairs are not settled here yet, and the King has only been a
few days in the realm. The Spaniards are hated, as I have seen in the past
and expect to see in the future. There was trouble at the last session of
5 Parliament . . . .
    On examining the brief sent hither by the Cardinal and intended to
dispense those who hold church property, I have noticed that it is not
drawn up in suitable manner. The Pope expects submission to the Church
to come first, and means afterwards to attend to the dispensations. . . . It
10 is my duty to inform your Majesty that the Catholics hold more church
property than do the heretics, and unless they obtain a general
dispensation to satisfy them that their titles will never be contested they
will not allow the Cardinal to execute his commission; and he will
certainly not be able to do so until the question has been submitted to
15 Parliament, former Acts of which have vested the title of Supreme Head
of the Church in the Crown, the right of which to deal with all religious
questions consequently stands firm. So if the Cardinal is to come here at
all, his powers had better be clear and comprehensive . . . (3 September
1554).

20   . . . Yesterday (29 November 1554) Parliament came to the unani-
mous decision that all the laws and statutes contrary to the Pope's
authority should be repealed, the Church's authority be once more
acknowledged, and the Cardinal admitted as legate to carry out his
mission . . . there was no hint of making conditions about Church
25   property, but only an expression of confidence that the King and Queen
would not allow that question to be handled in a manner likely to
compromise the attainment of the main object in view . . . .
        Simon Renard, the Imperial Ambassador, to the Emperor
        Charles v, *Calendar of State Papers, Spain 1554—8*, xiii, pp 45, 58

Questions

a   Identify 'Cardinal Pole' (line 1).
b   What, according to Renard, are the main obstacles to a reconciliation
      with Rome?
*   *c*   Account for the change in attitude of parliament towards the issue of
      reconciliation.
d   What evidence is there here that the queen was anxious 'to turn the
      clock back' to before 1529?
*   *e*   How did the king and queen handle the question of church property?

4 Persecution

The people of this town of London are murmuring about the cruel
enforcement of the recent acts of Parliament on heresy which has now
begun, as shown publicly when a certain Rogers was burnt yesterday.
Some of the onlookers wept, other prayed God to give them strength,
5   perseverance, and patience to bear the pain and not to recant, others
gathered the ashes and bones and wrapped them up in paper to preserve
them, yet others threatening the bishops. The haste with which the
bishops have proceeded in this matter may well cause a revolt. Although
it may seem necessary to apply exemplary punishment during your
10   Majesty's presence here and under your authority, and to do so before
winter is over to intimidate others, I do not think it well that your
Majesty should allow further executions to take place unless the reasons
are overwhelmingly strong and the offences committed have been so
scandalous as to render this course justifiable in the eyes of the people. I
15   think your Majesty would be wise to show firmness and to tell the bishops
that they are not to proceed to such lengths without having first consulted
you and the Queen. Otherwise, I forsee that the people may be
indisposed, although hitherto they have proved peaceable enough and
well disposed towards your Majesty. If this were to happen, which God
20   forbid and if the people got the upper hand, not only would the cause of
religion be again menaced, but the persons of your Majesty and the
Queen might be in peril. Your Majesty will also consider that the Lady

Elizabeth has her supporters, and that there are Englishmen who do not love foreigners. The nobility shows an altered countenance. The bishops
25 have their enemies, and so has the Chancellor (Gardiner) his. All these people grasp every occasion, especially with the approach of Spring. Your Majesty might inform the bishops that there are other means of chastising the obstinate, at this early stage: such as secret executions, banishment and imprisonment. The watchword should be *secure, caute et*
30 *lente festinare*. Indeed it is urgent to act in this sense, for I hear that the bishops intend to continue executions, and that other heretics are to be burnt this week, both in London and in the country.

> Simon Renard to Philip II, 5 February 1555, *Calender of State Papers, Spain 1554–8*, xiii, p 138

Questions

a Explain the reference to 'the recent acts of Parliament on heresy' (line 2).

b Who was 'a certain Rogers' (line 3)?

* *c* Who does Renard blame for the persecution? How have historians apportioned the blame?

d Why is Renard opposed to a policy of persecution?

* *e* Suggest reasons why the Marian persecution did *not* lead to revolt.

5 Martyrdom

(a) *Execution of Bishops Ridley and Latimer at Oxford, 16 October 1555*

Upon the north side of the town, in the ditch over against Balliol College, the place of execution was appointed. . . . Master doctor Ridley as he passed . . . looked up where master Cranmer did lie, hoping belike to have seen him at the glass window, and to have spoken unto him. But
5 then master Cranmer was busy . . . disputing . . . so that he could not see him.

Then Dr Smith . . . began his sermon to them upon this text of St. Paul, 'If I yield my body to the fire to be burnt, and have not charity, I shall gain nothing thereby'. . . . He cried to the people to beware of
10 them, for they were heretics and died out of the church. And . . . he declared their diversity in opinions as Lutherans, Zwinglians, of which sect they were he said, and that was the worst. . . . He ended with a very short exhortation to them to recant, and come home again to the church, and save their lives and souls, which else were condemned. . . . Then
15 they brought a faggot, kindled with fire, and laid the same down at Dr Ridley's feet. To whom master Latimer spoke in this manner: 'Be of good comfort, master Ridley, and play the man. We shall this day light such a candle, by God's grace, in England, as I trust shall never be put out' . . . .

> John Foxe, *Acts and Monuments*, 1843–9, Vol vii, p 547

(b) Execution of Agnes Potter and Joan Trunchfield of Ipswich

These two advocates and sufferers for the pure gospel of Jesus Christ, lived in the town of Ipswich, in Suffolk. Being apprehended on an information of heresy, they were brought before the bishop of Norwich, who examined them concerning their religion in general and their faith
5   in the corporeal presence of Christ in the sacrament of the altar in particular.

With respect to the latter article, they both delivered it as their opinion, that in the sacrament of the Lord's supper there was represented the memorial only of Christ's death and passion, saying that according to the
10 scriptures he was ascended up into heaven, and sat on the right hand of God the Father, and therefore his body could not be really and substantially in the sacrament.

A few days after this they were examined by the bishop, when, both of them still continuing steadfast in the profession of their faith, sentence was
15 pronounced against them as heretics, and they were delivered over to the secular power.

On the day appointed for their execution, which was in the month of March, 1556, they were both led to the stake and burnt, in the town of Ipswich. Their constancy was admired by the multitude who saw them suffer . . . .

John Foxe, *Acts and Monuments*, 1843–9, Vol xl, p 9

Questions

a   Comment on the reference to 'master Cranmer' (5(a) line 3).
b   Explain the reference to 'Lutherans' and 'Zwinglians' (5(a) line 11).
c   To what extent would these executions bear out the fears expressed by Simon Renard in the previous document?
d   'Sentence was pronounced against them as heretics and they were delivered over to the secular power.' (5(b) lines 13–14). Explain the process which culminated in the burning of a heretic.
* e   'One of the more unpalatable lessons of history is that persecution often works.' Was Mary's policy doomed to failure?
* f   'The work popularly known as Foxe's *Book of Martyrs* is the sole available source for the story. It is very far from being a really satisfactory source.' Why?

6   The Fate of Heretics: a Catholic View

. . . The facts are, that in the last four years of Mary's reign, between February 4, 1555, and November 10, 1558, something like 270 of her subjects were executed by burning, under laws which her government had revived, for the capital cause of obstinately adhering to beliefs that

5 contradicted the teaching of the Catholic Church, of which Church they
were all presumed to be members . . . .
   What is still the usual view of the horrible business and its immediate
effect has been vividly presented by a writer most sympathetic to Queen
Mary Tudor. Religious persecution, it is said, never doubted as a duty
10 and a wise policy, 'now became, not a principle taken for granted and
rarely applied, but a fact in the experience of gentle and simple alike.
Women at their marketing, men at their daily trade, the cobbler at his
bench, the ploughman trudging the furrow — all learnt to know the smell
of burning human flesh, the flesh of a neighbour, of a man or woman as
15 familiar as the parish pump. Mingling with the steam of washing day, or
with the reek of autumn bonfires, or polluting the sweetness of June, that
stench of human burning became a matter of everyday experience. Such
an experience, even in a cruel age, left behind it a memory and a
disgust. . . .' (H. F. M. Prescott).
20   Is this actually how the England of that time felt the Marian
persecution? Even that part of England where the heretics suffered? Will
the imaginative reconstruction stand when it is brought close to such
realities as the statistics, the geography of the executions, the mind of the
time about punishments, and about cruelty, and about the crime of
25 heresy? . . . .
   We must, if we wish to understand the matter at all, endeavour first to
reconstruct an age where, universally, the adherence to religious beliefs
considered as axiomatically false — and still more the propagation of such
beliefs — was held as one of the greatest of crimes . . . .
30   Did the news of these executions affect the people of that day as the
story of them affects us? There is much reason to doubt it; and the point is
worth notice . . . since it is an accepted commonplace with historians
that horror engendered in Mary's subjects by these executions was what
broke the last link binding the English people to their Catholic past . . . .
35   I suggest that, except in special localities, it may be the burnings had no
effect whatever; that for the mass of the nation the burnings were simply a
few more capital executions than usual — so few more, indeed, that the
increase on the year's total was in most places hardly perceptible . . . .
   General records of convictions and executions were not kept in the
40 sixteenth century, but a record has survived from the city of
Exeter. . . . From the assizes held there in 1598 . . . no fewer than
seventy-four convicts went to their death. 'If the number of executions in
each county was only twenty, or a little more than one quarter of the
number of capital sentences in Devonshire in 1598, this would make 800
45 executions a year in the forty English countries' (J. F. Stephen, 1888), this
of course in a country with a population only one fifteenth of what it is
today (1954). . . . If today we were habituated to the spectacle of
something like 12,000 executions yearly . . . we should hardly be
impressed as we assume our ancestors to have been, by the fact of an
50 additional number — comparatively small — now executed annually for
the crime called heresy.

Figures of burnings by years:

	1555	1556	1557	1558	Total
Sussex	4	13	10	0	27
Suffolk	3	8	2	9	22
Norfolk	3	0	4	3	10
Cambs. and Ely	2	1	0	0	3
Middlesex	3	0	4	6	13
Herts	3	0	0	0	3
London	7	16	13	10	46
Kent	21	7	26	5	59
Essex	16	21	12	3	52
Other areas[1]	10	17	4	1	32
Wales	2	0	0	1	3
TOTAL	74	83	75	38	270

1 Lichfield, 3; Coventry, 3; Leicester, 2; Northampton, 1; Derby, 1; Chester, 1; Bristol, 5; Gloucester, 3; Oxford, 3; Newbury, 3; Salisbury, 3; Wootton, 2; Banbury, 1; Exeter, 1

One striking fact about this violent attempt of Mary's government to stamp out doctrinal insubordination is that it was confined almost exclusively to London and the south-eastern counties . . . . Essex and
55 Kent were the counties which furnished most of the victims. Is it coincidence that these were the counties where, once the repressive hand of Henry VIII was lifted, the Anabaptist movement began to spread so extensively as to cause great alarm to Cranmer and his associates?. . . . Given the actual and projected persecution of the
60 'Anabaptists' in the years immediately preceeding Mary's accession, it is hard not to believe that there were many of these radical sectaries, against whom every man's hand was set, among the victims burnt in Essex and Kent during her reign . . . .
      From these two counties a good third of Foxe's martyrs – 111, came –
65 is it merely coincidence that of the most part of them he chronicles little but their names? . . . . It may be that of their beliefs he knew nothing at all. May it not be on the other hand that he knew that these unfortunates, very often, had belonged to sects universally reprobated? that they were men and women whose fate none would have pitied – had the beliefs for
70 which they were burnt been known, men and women whose deaths were no testimony to orthodox Protestantism and of no value as propaganda against Catholicism . . . .
      The cruelty of this particular punishment was but one detail of the general brutality of the age. . . . The heresy executions of the reign of
75 Mary Tudor no Catholic would not willingly forget . . . but they need to be remembered in all the fullness of their historical setting . . . .
      England surely was no longer a Catholic country by 1553.
. . . England was . . . a country that was very much the creation

of Henry VIII; plus a strong dosage of the religious beliefs and practices
80 that later came to be called Protestantism. . . . In this fact that England
has . . . become a country where so many of the people . . . have in fact
ceased to profess the Catholic faith, lies the real wickedness of the Marian
policy of executing heretics. . . . What happened in England in these
years . . . was not, in fact, the repression by a Catholic government of
85 heresy invading a Catholic country, but the repression of heresy by
Catholic *politiques* in a country where heresy had lately been fully
established, a country that is already in great part indifferent to religion:
and herein . . . lies the greatest scandal of the business, and the ultimate
reason why it was so easy to exploit it against Catholics in the generations
90 that followed, and to root it in so powerful an anti-Catholic tradition.

Philip Hughes, *The Reformation in England*, Vol II, 1954, pp 255,
261–2, 278, 280, 282–3, 286, 302–4

Questions

a   What arguments does Hughes put forward to counter the traditional
(protestant) interpretation of the Marian religious persecution? Are
you convinced by his arguments?

*   b   What factors (apart from the points made by Hughes) might account
for the large number of executions in London and the south-eastern
counties?

*   c   'Artisans and craftsmen make up 60 per cent of the convicted heretics
in the diocese of London whose social status is known to us, and this
pattern is similar to that which prevailed in other areas.' Comment.

d   Explain the references to (i) 'Anabaptist movement' (line 57) (ii)
'Catholic *politiques*' (line 86).

e   Why does Hughes condemn the Marian persecutions?

VII   Religion 1558–1603

Introduction

The Elizabethan religious settlement halted the English church somewhere between 'Rome and Geneva' though nearer to the latter than the
queen wished. Many Protestants, or 'puritans' as they were becoming
known, were bitterly disappointed with the settlement. The extremist
minority among them wanted a complete break with the past and in
particular the removal from the Prayer Book (1559) of all vestiges of
Roman influence, (e.g. the prescribed vestments, kneeling at communion). The less radical puritans though regarded such matters as
'adiaphora', 'things indifferent', and were prepared to accept them when
required to do so by properly constituted authority.

The early puritans did not form separate organisations or 'congre-
gations' but remained within the church. Because of this and because of
puritan strength in parliament and in convocation, the government could
only proceed against puritanism through the disciplinary authority of the
bishops, led initially by Archbishop Parker. This in turn produced firstly,
attacks on that authority; and secondly, the establishment, under the
influence of Thomas Cartwright and others, of independent 'presbyteries' or 'classes' to undermine and to bypass episcopal authority.

Elizabeth interpreted attacks on episcopal authority as attacks on the
crown which had appointed the bishops. Archbishop Grindal was
suspended for sympathising with the presbyterian or classical movement.
But under Archbishop Whitgift from 1583, and more particularly
because of the work of the ecclesiastical High Commission under
Richard Bancroft from 1593, the presbyteries were stamped out; and
only a minority, the 'Brownists', chose to suffer expulsion from their
livings rather than surrender their principles. Puritanism was not dead, as
the Stuarts were to discover, but it was contained by the end of Elizabeth's
reign.

Catholic 'recusants' were to constitute a greater threat to the
Elizabethan regime than the puritans. They were those Catholics,
probably only a few thousand, whose loyalty to the pope was stronger
than their sense of duty to the Crown. Probably in 1558 the majority of
English people were 'catholic' in the Henrician sense that they were
conservative in their religious views but that their principal allegiance

was to the Crown. The recusants, however, utterly rejected the Elizabethan settlement; they could not accept Elizabeth as their 'Supreme Governor', nor even, in some cases, as their rightful queen.

Prior to 1569–70 recusancy scarcely existed on any measurable scale. But when in 1570 the papal bull, 'Regnans in Excelsis', made treason obligatory for true Catholics; and when from 1574 Jesuit and seminary priests embarked upon their attempts to re-convert England, the government could no longer ignore the catholic threat, linked as it was to political dangers abroad. In 1581 recusancy fines were raised to £20 per month; and by 1585 the mere presence of catholic priests in England was made treasonable. Elizabeth's savage persecution – every bit as harsh as that of her predecessor – allied to the defeat of the Crown's catholic enemies, enabled the catholic threat, which had assumed menacing proportions between 1569 and 1588, to be brought firmly under control before the end of the reign.

Further Reading

To supplement studies of the Elizabethan religious settlement and its consequences in the standard text books and biographies see the stimulating, and sometimes provocative, sections in, A. G. Dickens, *The English Reformation* (1972) chaps 12 and 13; Claire Cross, *Church and People, 1450–1660* (1976) chap. 6; Conrad Russell, *The Crisis of Parliaments, 1509–1660* (1971) chap. 3; G. W. O. Woodward, *Reformation and Resurgence* (1963) chaps 7 and 8; W. R. D. Jones, *The Mid-Tudor Crisis, 1539–63* (1973) chap. 4 (part of which is quoted below, see pp 89–91); D. M. Loades, *Politics and the Nation, 1450–1660* (1974) pp. 250– 57, 277–93; M. M. Reese, *The Puritan Impulse, 1559–1660* (1975); Patrick McGrath, *Papists and Puritans under Elizabeth I* (1967); P. Collinson, *The Elizabethan Puritan Movement* (1967); C. Hill, *Reformation to Industrial Revolution* (1974) pp 112–13 offers a Marxist interpretation of the scene – 'Puritanism was a knife and fork question'. For the rebellion of 1569 see Anthony Fletcher, *Tudor Rebellions* (1968).

1 The Religious Situation in England, December 1558–May 1559

December 15, 1558   It gives me great trouble every time I write to your Majesty not to be able to send more pleasing intelligence, but what can be expected from a country governed by a queen, and she a young lass, who, although sharp, is without prudence, and is every day standing up against 5 religion more openly? . . . .

December 29   On the Sunday of Christmastime the queen before going to mass sent for the bishop of Carlisle who was to officiate, and told him that he need not elevate the host for adoration . . . . This affair is going at a pace that, in spite of the good offices your Majesty may perform with

10 the pope, it will be impossible to stop, and I hear that he will declare this
    queen a bastard and will proceed against her, giving the right to the
    crown to the queen of Scots . . . .

    February 20, 1559 . . . I think it will be well for your Majesty's
    commissioners to speak with the queen's commissioners on this subject of
15 religion, and express their sorrow at the wickedness which is being
    planned in this parliament, which consists of persons chosen throughout
    the country as being the most perverse and heretical . . . . That accursed
    cardinal left twelve bishoprics to be filled, which will now be given to as
    many ministers of Lucifer instead of being worthily bestowed . . . .

20 March 19 These heretics and the devil that prompts them are so careful
    to leave no stone unturned to compass their ends that no doubt they have
    persuaded her that your Majesty wishes to marry her for religious objects
    alone, and so she kept repeating to me that she was heretical and
    consequently could not marry your Majesty. She was so disturbed and
25 excited and so resolved to restore religion as her father left it, that at last I
    said that I . . . could not believe that she would sanction the things which
    were being discussed in parliament . . . .
        She said she would not take the title of head of the church, but that so
    much money was taken out of the country for the Pope every year that
30 she must put an end to it . . . . I replied that . . . (it) was a great scandal
    that so many rogues should come from Germany, and get into the pulpit
    before her . . . .

    May 10 The news here is that parliament closed the day before
    yesterday . . . and the queen having confirmed what had been
35 adopted . . . she now remains governess of the Anglican church . . . . It
    is a great pity to see what is going on here. From Easter they will begin to
    say the service everywhere in English, and they have already commenced
    to do so in the queen's chapel. They tell me everything is worse even than
    in the time of King Edward . . . .
            Count de Feria, the Spanish Ambassador, to Philip II, *Calendar of*
            State Papers, Spanish, 1558–1567, i, pp 7–67

Questions

a   What is it possible to learn from these extracts about the religious
    situation in England in the first six months of Elizabeth's reign?
b   What do these extracts reveal about Spanish policy at this time?
c   Comment on the view of parliament revealed in lines 16–17.
d   Identify 'that accursed cardinal' (line 18). How many new bishops
    was Elizabeth able to appoint and what were the consequences?
e   'She was . . . resolved to restore religion as her father left it' (lines
    24–5). Is this an accurate assessment of Elizabeth's policy?
f   What hint is there is these extracts that Elizabeth had to accept a more
    radical settlement than she had intended?

2 An Act restoring to the Crown the ancient jurisdiction over the State ecclesiastical and spiritual, and abolishing all foreign power repugnant to the same, 1559

V   . . . May it also please your Highness that it may be enacted that one Act and Statute made in the first year of the late King Edward the Sixth . . . intituled an Act against such persons as shall unreverently speak against the Sacrament of the Body and Blood of Christ, commonly
5 called the Sacrament of the Altar, and for the receiving thereof under both kinds . . . shall and may likewise from the last day of this session of Parliament be revived . . . .
VII   To the intent that all usurped and foreign power and authority, spiritual and temporal, may for ever be clearly extinguished . . . may it
10 be enacted . . . that no foreign prince, person, prelate, state or potentate . . . shall . . . enjoy or exercise any manner of power . . . within this realm . . . but . . . the same shall be clearly abolished out of this realm . . . for ever . . . .
VIII   . . . such jurisdictions . . . spiritual and ecclesiastical . . . (shall)
15 be united and annexed to the imperial crown of this realm; and . . . your Highness, your heirs and successors . . . shall have full power . . . to visit, reform, redress, order, correct and amend all such heresies, errors, schisms, abuses, offences, contempts and enormities whatsoever, which by any manner of spiritual or ecclesiastical power, authority or
20 jurisdiction, can or may be lawfully reformed . . . .
IX   And for the better observation and maintenance of this Act . . . may it be further enacted . . . that all . . . and every ecclesiastical person and . . . officer and minister . . . and all and every temporal judge . . . lay or temporal officer or minister, and every other person
25 having your Highness' fee or wages . . . shall make, take and receive a corporal oath . . . .
   I, A.B., do utterly testify and declare in my conscience, that the Queen's Highness is the only supreme governor of this realm and of all other her Highness' dominions and countries, as well in all spiritual or
30 ecclesiastical things or causes as temporal . . . .
            1 Eliz. c. 1 *Statutes of the Realm*, lv, pt. i, 351

Questions

a By what name is this act better known?
b Comment on the wording of the title of the act.
c What are the implications of article V?
d 'Supreme Governor was but Supreme Head writ large.' Comment on this contemporary view of the new title.

3 An Act for the Uniformity of Common Prayer and Divine Service in the Church and the Administration of the Sacraments 1559

Where at the death of our late sovereign lord King Edward the Sixth there remained one uniform order of common Service and Prayer and of the administration of Sacraments, rites and ceremonies in the Church of England, which was set forth in one book entitled *The Book of Common*
5 *Prayer* . . . authorised by act of parliament holden in the fifth and sixth years of our late sovereign lord . . . the which was repealed in the first year of the reign of . . . Queen Mary. . . . Be it therefore enacted . . . that the said book, with the order of service, and of the administration of sacraments, rites and ceremonies, with the alterations and additions
10 therein added and appointed by this statute, shall stand and be . . . in full force and effect . . . .
II And be it further enacted . . . that all and singular ministers . . . shall . . . be bounden to say and use . . . the said book . . . with one alteration or addition of certain Lessons . . . and the form of the
15 Litany altered and corrected, and two sentences only added in the delivery of the sacrament to the communicants . . . .
III And it is ordained and enacted that . . . every person inhabiting within this realm . . . shall diligently and faithfully, having no lawful or reasonable excuse to be absent, endeavour themselves to resort to their
20 parish church or chapel accustomed . . . and there to abide orderly and soberly during the time of the Common Prayer . . . upon pain that every person so offending shall forfeit for every offence twelve pence to be levied by the churchwardens of the parish where such offence shall be done, to the use of the poor of the same parish, of the goods, lands and
25 tenements of such offender, by way of distress . . . .
XIII Provided always . . . that such ornaments of the Church and of the ministers thereof shall be retained and in use, as was in the Church of England . . . in the second year of the reign of King Edward . . . until other order shall be therein taken . . . and also that, if there shall happen
30 any contempt or irreverence to be used in the ceremonies or rites of the Church by the misusing of the orders appointed in this book, the queen's majesty may . . . ordain and publish further ceremonies or rites . . . .
1 Eliz. c. 2 *Statutes of the Realm*, lv, pt. i, 355

Questions

a Which Prayer book was re-introduced in 1559?
* b What 'alterations and additions' (line 9) were made?
c What was the aim of article III?
d Give examples of what was meant by 'ornaments of the Church and of the ministers' (lines 26– 7), and 'ceremonies or rites of the Church' (lines 30– 1). Why did article XIII provoke opposition?

4 Puritan Demands in the Lower House of Convocation 1563

I That all the Sundays in the year and principal feasts of Christ be kept holidays and all other holidays to be abrogated.

II That in all parish churches the minister in common prayer turn his face toward the people, and there distinctly read the divine service
5 appointed, where all the people assembled may hear and be edified.

III That in ministering the sacrament of baptism the ceremony of making the Cross in the child's forehead may be omitted as tending to superstition.

IV That, forasmuch as divers communicants are not able to kneel
10 during the time of the communion for age, sickness and sundry other infirmities, and some also superstitiously both kneel and knock, that order of kneeling to be left to the discretion of the ordinary within his jurisdiction.

V That it be sufficient for the minister in time of saying divine service
15 and ministering the sacraments, to use a surplice, and that no minister say service or minister the sacraments but in a comely garment or habit.

VI That the use of organs be removed.

John Strype, *Annals*, 1735, I, p 502

Questions

a Summarise the demands of the Puritans set out above.

b These articles were rejected by one vote – 59 against, 58 for. What does this suggest?

c Which of the articles above was to become most closely associated with puritanism?

* d What other traditional puritan demands are *not* included in this list?

5 (a) The Lack of Uniformity

Some say the service in the chancel, others in the body of the church; some say the same in a seat made in the church, some in the pulpit with their faces to the people; some keep precisely the order of the book, others intermeddle psalms in metre; some say in a surplice, others without a
5 surplice; the table standeth in the body of the church in some places, in others it standeth in the chancel; in some places the table standeth altarwise, distant from the wall a yard, in some others in the middle of the chancel, north and south; in some places the table is joined; in others it standeth upon trestles; in some places the table hath a carpet, in others it
10 hath not; administration of the Communion is done by some with surplice and cap, some with surplice alone, others with none; some with chalice, others with a Communion cup, others with a common cup; some with unleavened bread, some with leavened; some receive kneeling,

others standing, others sitting; some baptise in a font, some in a basin;
15 some sign with the sign of the cross, others sign not. Apparel – some with
a square cap, some with a round cap, some with a button cap, some with a
hat.

> *Summary of the returns from the dioceses submitted to William Cecil in*
> *1564,* quoted in M. M. Reese, *The Puritan Impulse, 1559–1660,*
> 1975, p 100

5 (b) Archbishop Parker's *Advertisements* 1566

The Queen's Majesty, of her godly zeal calling to remembrance how
necessary it is to the advancement of God's glory . . . for all her loving
subjects . . . to be knit together in one perfect unity of doctrine and to be
conjoined in one uniformity of rites and manners . . . hath straitly
5 charged (the Archbishop of Canterbury) that, with assistance and
conference had with other bishops, namely such as be in commission
for causes ecclesiastical, some order might be taken whereby all
diversities . . . among them of the clergy and the people . . . might be
reformed . . . Whereupon . . . these orders and rules ensuing have been
10 thought meet and convenient to be used and followed; not yet
prescribing these rules as laws . . . but as temporal orders mere
ecclesiastical . . . and as rules in some part of discipline concerning
decency, distinction and order for the time . . . .

II. *Articles for administration of prayers and sacraments.*
15 (2) Item, That no parson or curate, not admitted by the bishop of the
diocese to preach, do expound in his own cure or otherwise any scripture
or matter of doctrine . . . but only study to read . . . the homilies
already set out . . . .
(6) Item, That every minister saying any public prayers or ministering
20 the sacraments or other rites of the church shall wear a comely surplice
with sleeves, to be provided at the charges of the parish; and that the
parish provide a decent table standing on a frame for a communion table.
(8) That all communicants do receive kneeling . . . .

> Printed in G. W. Prothero, *Select Statutes and other Constitutional*
> *Documents,* 1913, pp 192–3

Questions

a Did the lack of uniformity revealed in the dioceses concern ritual or
doctrine, or both?
b Why were Parker's *Advertisements* not prescribed as laws (5(b)
lines 10–11)?
* *c* Comment on the origins and the powers of the 'commission for causes
ecclesiastical' (5(b) lines 6–7).
* *d* What were 'the homilies already set out' (5(b) lines 17–18)? Why
was great emphasis placed on what was preached? How, and with what

consequences, did the Puritans try to improve the standard of
preaching?

*   *e*   Parker believed that many of the faults set out in extract 5(a) were
'adiaphora': why then did he pursue a policy of uniformity and what
were the dangers of this policy?

6   The Papal Bull of Deposition 1570

. . . Elizabeth . . . after she had gained the throne, usurped to herself
monstrously the place of supreme head of the Church in all England and
the principal authority and jurisdiction in it. . . . She has taken away by a
violent hand the use of true religion which had previously been over-
5   thrown by the apostate Henry VIII . . . she has followed and embraced
the errors of heretics . . . . She has oppressed holders of the Catholic
faith . . . . She has abolished the sacrifice of the mass, prayers, fastings,
choice of foods, celibacy, and Catholic rites; she has commanded books
which contain manifest heresy to be spread through the whole kingdom;
10   she has required services which are impious and instituted according to
the prescriptions of Calvin to be accepted . . . observed . . . and acknowledged by her subjects . . . .
     She has compelled by an oath very many to agree to her wicked laws
and to abjure the authority and obedience of the Roman pontiff, and to
15   recognise her alone as mistress in temporal and spiritual affairs. . . . And
so . . . we declare the aforesaid Elizabeth a heretic and a favourer of
heretics, and those who adhere to her in the aforesaid matter, to have
incurred the sentence of anathema, and to be cut off from the unity of the
body of Christ. Moreover she is deprived of her pretended right to the
20   kingdom. . . . Likewise the nobles, subjects and people of the said
kingdom . . . (are) absolved perpetually for the future from all duty,
fidelity and obedience due . . . and we require and order . . . all . . . not
to venture to obey her instructions, mandates, or laws . . . .
     Given at Rome, at St. Peter's, in the year of the Lord's incarnation,
25   1570 (February) . . . in the fifth year of our pontificate (Pius V).
     Dodd's Church History of England, ed. M. A. Tierney, 1839–43,
     Vol III, App. pp ii ff

Questions

*   *a*   How would you account for the timing of the papal bull of 1570?
     b   Of what 'crimes' is Elizabeth accused?
     c   What sentence was pronounced against Elizabeth?
*   *d*   'The papal damp squib'. Comment on this view of the bull of 1570.
*   *e*   How did the English government react to the papal bull?

7 **The 'Bloody Questions' submitted to English Catholics to test their loyalty, and the answers of Henry Orton and John Hart (no date)**[1]

1. *Whether the bull of Pius V against the queen's Majesty be a lawful sentence, and ought to be obeyed by the subjects of England?*

Orton: To the first he sayth that he thinketh the bull of Pius V was at no time a lawful sentence, or of force to binde any of her Majestie's
5 subjects, and that notwithstanding, her Majestie was and is to be obeyed by every of her subjects.

Hart: To the first he saith, that it is a difficult question, and that he cannot make answere thereto.

3 *Whether the pope has, or had, power to authorize the earls of*
10 *Northumberland, Westmoreland, and others of her Majesty's subjects, to rebel, or take arms against her Majesty. . . . ?*

Orton: . . . He thinketh the pope neither hath nor had authoritie to warrant any of the persons here named . . . or any other of her subjects, to take armes against her Majestie . . . .
15 *Hart*: . . . He cannot answere, and further saith, that he will not meddle with any such questions.

4 *Whether the pope hath power to discharge any of her Highness' subjects . . . from their allegiance . . . to her Majesty. . . . ?*

Orton: . . . He thinketh the pope hath no authoritie to discharge any
20 subject from his allegiance . . . .

Hart: . . . He saith, he is not resolved, and therefore he cannot answere.

6 *If the pope do by his bull or sentence pronounce her Majesty to be deprived and no lawful queen, and her subjects to be discharged of their allegiance and obedience unto her, and, after the pope or any other of his appointment and*
25 *authority do invade this realm, which part would you take, or which part ought a good subject of England to take?*

Orton: . . . He sayth, that in the case here supposed, he would take part with her Majestie against the pope, or any other invading the realm by his authoritie.
30 *Hart*: . . . He saith, that when such a case shall happen, he will then advise what becommeth him to do, for presently he is not resolved.

Dodd's Church History of England, ed. M. A. Tierney, 1839–43, Vol III, App. pp iv–xvi

1 In 1564 the Council of Trent had re-affirmed that all Catholics were to owe obedience to the papacy. The questions began to be regularly applied after 1580.

Questions

a What are these questions seeking to prove?

b Explain the reference to the 'earls of Northumberland, (and) Westmoreland' (lines 9–10). Why was there so little catholic opposition to Elizabeth?
c Was Henry Orton both a loyal subject and a good Catholic?
d Was John Hart disloyal?
e How did English Catholics react when 'such a case' (line 30) *did* happen?

8 Presbyterian Demands 1572

Seeing that nothing in this mortal life is more diligently to be sought for and carefully to be looked unto than the restitution of true religion and reformation of God's church: it shall be your parts (dearly beloved) in this present Parliament assembled, as much as in you lieth to promote the
5 same, and to employ your whole labour and study, not only in abolishing all papish remnants both in ceremonies and regiment but also in bringing in and placing in God's church those things only which the Lord Himself in His word commandeth. . . . May it therefore please your wisdom to understand, we in England are so far off from having a church rightly
10 reformed according to the prescript of God's word, that as yet we are not come to the outward face of the same . . . . In those days no idolatrous sacrificers or heathenish priests were appointed to be preachers of the Gospel: but we allow . . . papish mass-mongers, men for all seasons, King Henry's priests, King Edward's priests, Queen Mary's priests, who
15 of truth (if God's word were precisely followed) should from the same be utterly removed . . . . Then election was made by the common consent of the whole church: now everyone picketh out for himself some notable good benefice . . . . Titles, livings, and offices by Anti Christ devised are given to them as Metropolitan, Archbishop, Lord's Grace, Lord Bishop,
20 Suffragan, Dean, Archdeacon . . . all which . . . as they are strange and unheard of in Christ's Church, nay, plainly in God's word forbidden, so are they utterly with speed out of the same to be removed . . . to bring in that old and true election which was accustomed to be made by the congregation. . . . Appoint to every congregation a learned and diligent
25 preacher. . . . Take away the lordship, the loitering, the pomp, the idleness and livings of Bishops. . . . To . . . Ministers, Seniors and Deacons is the whole regiment of the church to be committed. . . . Not that we mean to take away the authority of the civil Magistrate and chief Governor, to whom we wish all blessedness . . . but that Christ being
30 restored into his Kingdom . . . the Prince may be better obeyed . . . .
    . . . Is a reformation good for France? and can it be evil for England? Is discipline meet for Scotland? and is it unprofitable for this realm? Surely God hath set these examples before your eyes to encourage you to go forward to a thorough and speedy reformation. You may not do as
35 heretofore you have done, patch and piece, nay rather go backward and never labour or contend to perfection. But altogether remove whole Anti

Christ, both head, body and branch, and perfectly plant that purity of the word, that simplicity of the sacraments, and severity of discipline, which Christ hath commended and commanded to His church.

John Field and Thomas Wilcox, *An Admonition to the Parliament*, 1572, in *Puritan Manifestoes*, ed. Frere and Douglas, pp 8—19

Questions

*   a   Account for the timing of this *Admonition*, and in what circumstances was it issued?

     b   What form of church government did Presbyterians want?

     c   'Not that we mean to take away the authority of the civil magistrate' (line 28). Comment on this statement.

     d   Explain the references to 'France' and 'Scotland' (lines 31—2).

*   e   How, and with what success, did the government deal with the Presbyterians?

     f   Compare these presbyterian demands of 1572 with the puritan demands of 1563 (extract 4 in this section). What are the differences between them?

9   Execution of William Hart[1] 1583

. . . Being fastened down upon the hurdle, he was drawn through the streets to the place of execution . . . . Before he came to the gallows, he was met by two ministers, Mr Bunny and Mr Price, who made it their business to affront him, and to persuade the people that he did not die for
5   his religion, but for treason. As soon as he arrived at the place, he cheerfully went up the ladder, and began to pray in silence. They ask'd him if he prayed for the queen. He answered, that he had always prayed for her to that day, and as long as he lived would not cease to pray for her; that he willingly acknowledged her for his sovereign, and professed a
10   ready obedience to her, in all things which were not inconsistent with the Catholic religion.

Then Mr Bunny step'd out and read aloud . . . the bull of Pius v; by which he had excommunicated the queen, etc., pretending to prove that Mr Hart must needs be a traitor; and that the business of his coming over
15   was to withdraw her Majesty's subjects from their allegiance. Mr Hart answered, in short, that far from having any such thoughts, he had ever prayed for the queen's safety, and the happy state of the kingdom . . . . He was . . . interrupted by the ministers, calling upon him to join with them in prayer, which he refused to do, telling them that
20   his faith and theirs was not the same. But he desired the Catholics to pray for him, and to bear witness that he died in and for the Catholic faith, and not for any crime whatsoever, or treason against the state. With that he was thrown off the ladder; and, according to sentence was cut down alive and quarter'd . . . .

Richard Challoner, *Memoirs of Missionary Priests*, Vol 1, 1924, pp
123–4

1 William Hart, a seminary priest, educated at Douai, Rheims and Rome, returned to
England for missionary work and was executed at York in 1583.

Questions

a Explain the reference to 'the business of his coming over' (line 14).
b 'He did not die for his religion, but for *treason*' (lines 4–5). Comment
   on this view.
* c How did the Elizabethan government deal with the problems posed
     by the influx of Jesuit and seminary priests?
* d How many Catholics were executed by Elizabeth? Why did these
     executions not arouse the horror which is associated with the Marian
     persecution?
* e 'By the time she went to war with the Champion of the Counter
     Reformation, England was a protestant country in a sense which she
     had certainly not been in 1550, in 1559, or even in 1569.' What
     developments since 1569 had brought this about?

10   The Elizabethan Religious Settlement: 'the highest common denominator'?

. . . It is suggested that the Queen did not intend to frame a full and final
settlement in the first session of Parliament in 1559; she wanted to wipe
out the Marian legislation and to restore the position obtaining in the first
year of the reign of Edward VI, but as yet desired neither a prayer book
5   nor an act of uniformity. But her policy was modified by circumstances.
Professor Hurstfield suggests that 'as in other crises of her reign, Elizabeth
did not start off with any clear solution in mind but rescued compromise
out of a dangerous situation'.[1] The dangers of the position, and the nature
and balance of that compromise, derived from the almost complete non-
10 compliance of the Marian upper clergy on the one hand, and the strength
of Protestant sympathies and influence on returning émigrés in
Parliament (to which she was forced to turn) on the other . . . .
    Thus the first and very limited 'bill to restore the supremacy of the
Church of England to the Crown of the realm' and (almost certainly) to
15 re-establish Communion in both kinds, introduced to the Commons in
early February, emerged from the committee stage a much-extended and
explicitly Protestant document – Sir John Neale conjectures that it
'revived the 1552 Prayer Book and re-established the religious structure
as it was at the death of Edward VI'.[2] In March the Lords effectively
20 restored it to its previous form, but the Commons' reluctant acceptance
was followed not by the expected royal signature but by adjournment of
Parliament until 3 April. It has been contended that the international
recognition accorded to Elizabeth by the terms of the Treaty of Cateau-

Cambrésis, news of which reached England on 19 March, emboldened
25 her to take a more positive line and led to a more definitive set of
proposals; but one historian[3] has asked the pertinent question: 'Why
would the news have thrown Elizabeth into the arms of the eager
reformers?' The answer may be that the news, together with the evidence
of the extent and depth of feeling in the Lower House of Parliament,
30 encouraged the more Protestant members of her Council (perhaps Cecil,
Bacon and Knollys) to urge upon the Queen the safety and the wisdom of
a compromise which went some way towards meeting the sweeping
demands of the Commons' amendments and counter-proposals. For
whatever reason there seems little doubt that, in the event, the settlement
35 came rather more quickly and went significantly further in a Protestant
direction than the Queen herself would have wished.

In April 1559 a third and government sponsored bill was introduced
which, restoring the royal supremacy with a change of title which has
been variously interpreted as a concession to Catholics and Calvinists,
40 described the Queen as 'supreme governor as well in all spiritual or
ecclesiastical things or causes as temporal' . . . . This measure passed
rapidly through the Commons and, despite debate in the Lords and
indeed its rejection by all the spiritual peers reached statutory form as the
Act of Supremacy by the end of the month. Professor Dickens[4] has
45 observed that the change in title accorded to the Queen was no mere
quibble but reflected realities, for 'Parliament was becoming a co-
ordinate power rather than an agent . . . .' An 'Act for the Uniformity of
common prayer and divine service . . . and the administration of the
sacraments' soon followed. The Book of Common Prayer described
50 therein was the product of another compromise. It went far nearer to that
of 1552 than Elizabeth (whose preference was for the version of 1549)
would have wished; yet, the 'Black Rubric' was deleted, while
conciliation in regard to the nature of the Eucharist was attempted by the
device of including the wording of both the Edwardian Prayer Books at
55 the crucial point in its celebration. The clergy were to conform upon pain
of fine, imprisonment and deprivation, while the Queen's subjects were
all to attend Church under penalty of a fine of 12d per absence. Clause
XIII decreed 'that such ornaments of the Church and of the Ministers shall
be retained and be in use as was in the Church of England by authority of
60 Parliament in the second year of King Edward the Sixth'. This clear
indication of the Queen's own tenacity of purpose was to prove
contentious. Yet V. J. K. Brooks[5] sees it as a tribute to Elizabeth's
statecraft in that as far as the majority of her subjects were concerned
it represented a well-judged conciliatory measure. . . . 'To maintain
65 clerical vestments and customary ceremonial, even at a reduced level, was
the surest way to advertise the continuity of the church in England against
Swiss innovation. (Indeed) to have given way about vestments would
probably have offended far more than it would have appeased, and
would have destroyed all hope of a national church.'
70 The settlement of 1559 was, in effect, the result of a compromise

between the Queen's own wish for comprehension and the pressures of the returning émigrés. Patrick McGrath[6] describes it as representing 'the highest common denominator among the various Protestant groups'. As such it glossed over tensions which were never to be completely resolved, and established an equilibrium which at the time must have appeared both provisional and precarious. Yet it was to endure as the permanent basis of the English Church.

75

> Whitney R. D. Jones, *The Mid-Tudor Crisis 1539–1563*, 1973, pp 106–9

1   J. Hurstfield, *Elizabeth I and the Unity of England* (1960) p 32
2   J. E. Neale, *Elizabeth I and her Parliaments* (1953) I, pp 57–8
3   W. P. Haugaard, *Elizabeth and the English Reformation* (1968) pp 98–9
4   A. G. Dickens, *The English Reformation* (1972) pp 302–3
5   V. J. K. Brook, *Whitgift and the English Church* (1957) p 21
6   P. McGrath, *Papists and Puritans under Elizabeth I* (1967) p 13

Questions

a 'Protestant doctrine for the intellectuals, catholic ceremonies for the masses'; 'It was a bargain but not a compromise'; 'A compromise in which the queen conceded most'; 'Hardly a compromise at all'; 'A total victory for the queen': in what senses was the Elizabethan church settlement a 'compromise'?

b What were the reasons for, and what evidence is there to suggest that the settlement went 'significantly further in a Protestant direction' than Elizabeth wanted?

* *c* Which element of the settlement, in your opinion, most clearly reflects its compromise nature?

* *d* What reasons, apart from those given in the extract, have been put forward to explain the queen's title of 'Supreme Governor'?

* *e* Was the settlement a tolerant settlement?

* *f* Why was there so little opposition to the Elizabethan settlement?

VIII   Parliament 1558–1603

Introduction

By the sixteenth century parliament had become an accepted, though not a regular, part of the constitution. It was taken for granted that parliaments would meet only occasionally, for specific purposes, usually for the granting of money. The reign of Elizabeth I was no exception; indeed her reign has been described as a period of efficient conciliar government, with resort to parliaments only when they could not be avoided. It must not be presumed that Elizabeth was making a deliberate attempt to suppress parliament: like her predecessors she never supposed that she would never call another parliament.

In her near forty-five-year reign there were ten parliaments with thirteen sessions which met for a sum total of about 140 weeks. All parliaments, except the first, were held to secure money. On average there was a parliamentary session every $3\frac{1}{2}$ years; the longest gap between sessions occurred between 1576 and 1581. There were no parliaments in twenty-nine of the forty-five years, and clearly parliament was an intermittent institution.

Contemporary commentators bear this out. 'What can a commonwealth desire more than peace, liberty, quietness, little taking of base money, and few parliaments . . . ', wrote Sir Thomas Smith in 1560. 'Her Majesty', said the Lord Keeper in 1593, 'hath evermore been most loth to call for the assembly of the people in her parliament and hath done the same but rarely.'

During Elizabeth's reign the lower house evolved into the more important of the two houses of parliament. Her M.P.s still came from the same social background as M.P.s earlier in the century. They were landed gentry often closely related to the nobility – and Elizabeth's creation of thirty one new boroughs between 1559–86 increased the numbers of gentry in the Commons, who by 1586 accounted for 80 per cent of all M.P.s – but they were more ambitious, had a wider interest in national and international affairs and they were better educated than their predecessors. In 1563, 139 out of 420 M.P.s had had some form of higher education; in 1593 more than half (252) had been to a university and, or, the Inns of Court. In that age a good education often bred strong protestant convictions; and so it was that Elizabeth's parliaments came to contain a vociferous, articulate puritan element.

Peter Wentworth, the most famous M.P. of the period, was in many ways typical of the new breed. A wealthy landowner, related to the nobility, he was probably educated at Lincoln's Inn, and he was a patron of puritanism. His death in the Tower (1597), where he had been consigned for his beliefs, is a reminder that though, in the main, Elizabeth's parliaments were content to follow the government's lead, there was a strong radical – political and religious – element typified by Norton, Wentworth himself, Cope, Strickland and others, the puritan-minded gentlemen-lawyers who orchestrated the 'Puritan choir'. They sought by the expression of 'free speech', which they saw as a means to an end and not an end in itself, to bring about fundamental changes in church and state.

Against this threat from within Elizabeth struggled to maintain the delicate balance between Crown and Commons. She did not dare to veto too many bills. She chose rather to yield when necessary – as in 1559, 1586–7, 1601, – or, as over marriage and the succession, to prevaricate until it was too late. Her instruments in 'managing' the Commons were her privy councillors – never before and never again was the privy council so efficient in this respect – and the Speaker, always under the Tudors a royal nominee. Except in the crisis of 1601 they served her well.

' . . . Yet this I account the glory of my crown', Elizabeth could say after this stormy episode, 'that I have reigned with your loves.' Her 'Golden Speech' was no empty flattery of the Commons. It symbolises rather the essential unity between Crown and Commons (Neale's 'strange fundamental harmony'), between the Queen and her people, which still existed at the end of her reign. However much they might have disagreed Elizabeth had not lost the respect and general approbation of her parliament.

Further Reading

R. K. Gilkes, *The Tudor Parliament* (1969) is a useful introduction with good bibliographies. Sir John Neale's famous trilogy still colours everything written on this topic: *The Elizabethan House of Commons* (1949); *Elizabeth I and her Parliaments, 1559–1581* (1953); and *Elizabeth I and her Parliaments, 1584–1601* (1957). See also Neale, *Essays in Elizabethan History* (1958). G. R. Elton, *The Tudor Constitution* (1960) part 8, pp 228–317, contains introductory essays and illustrative documentary material on the Tudor parliament in general and the Elizabethan scene in particular. Fryde and Miller (eds) *Historical Studies of the English Parliament*, Vol 2, 1399–1603 (1970) reprints a number of seminal articles and has a valuable introduction. The debate on 'Tudor Despotism' (see p. 102) can be followed in J. Hurstfield, 'Was there a Tudor Despotism after all?' TRHS (1967) 5th series Vol 17, pp 83–103 (now conveniently reprinted in J. Hurstfield, *Freedom, Corruption and Government in Elizabethan England* (1973), pp 23–49); and G. R. Elton, 'The Rule of Law in Sixteenth-Century England' in *Studies in Tudor and Stuart Politics and Government*, Vol 1 (1974) pp 260–84.

1 Parliament: Composition and Powers

(a) The House of Lords:

The first day of the parliament the Prince and all the lordes in their robes of parliament do meet in this higher house. . . . Next under the prince sitteth the Chancellor, who is the voyce and orator of the prince. On one side of the house or chamber sitteth the archbishops and bishops . . . on
5 the other side the dukes and barons. In the middest thereof uppon woolsackes sitteth the Judges of the realme, the master of the roules, and the secretaries of estate. But these that sit on woolsackes have no voice in the house, but only sit there to answere their knowledge in the law.

(b) The House of Commons:

In this meantime the knights of the shire and the burgesses of the
10 parliament . . . are called by such as it pleaseth the prince to appoint . . . to which they answere and declaring for what shire or towne they answere: then they are willed to choose an able man to be the mouth of them all, and to present him . . . to the prince: which donne . . . the chancellor in the prince's name doth so much declare him
15 able . . . and thanketh the commons for choosing so wise, discreete and eloquent a man, and willeth them to go and consult of the laws for the commonwealth.

(c) The most high and absolute power of the realm of England consisteth in the Parliament. For as in war, where the King himself in person, the
20 nobility, the rest of the gentility and the yeomanry are, is the force and power of England: so in peace and consultation where the prince is to give life and the last and highest commandment, the barony for the nobility and higher, the knights esquires, gentlemen and commons for the lower part of the commonwealth, consult and show what is good and necessary
25 for the commonwealth, and to consult together and upon mature deliberation (every bill or law being thrice read and disputed upon in either House) the other two parts first each part and after the prince himself in presence of both the parts doth consent unto and alloweth. That is the prince's and whole realm's deed; whereupon justly no man can
30 complain but must accommodate himself to find it good and obey it. That which is done by this consent . . . is taken for law . . . . For every Englishman is intended to be there present, either in person or by procuration and attorneys, of what preeminence, state, dignity or quality soever he be, from the prince . . . to the lowest person in England. And
35 the consent of the Parliament is taken to be every man's consent.

> Sir Thomas Smith, *De Republica Anglorum*, 1565, ed. L. Alston, 1906, pp 48–52

Questions

a What three elements constitute 'Parliament'?
b Who were the officials who sat on the woolsacks in the Lords?

* c Who were the 'burgesses'? What could be deduced from the following: (i) their numbers increased by sixty-two under Elizabeth, (ii) by c.1600 two boroughs out of three were represented by two non-residents?

d How was statute law being made by the 1560s?

e Comment on the view that 'The most high and absolute power of the realm of England consisteth in the Parliament' (lines 18–19).

2 (a) Customary Demand for the Privileges of the House of Commons

. . . Further, I am to be a suitor to your Majesty that, when matters of importance shall arise whereupon it shall be necessary to have your Highness' opinion, that then I may have free access unto you for the same: and the like to the Lords of the Upper House.

5 Secondly, that in repairing from the Nether House to your Majesty or the lords to the Upper House, to declare their meanings, and I mistaking or uttering the same contrary to their meaning, that then my fault or imbecility in declaring thereof be not prejudicial to the House, but that I may again repair to them, the better to understand their meanings and so
10 they to reform the same.

Thirdly, that the assembly of the lower House may have frank and free liberties to speak their minds without any controlment, blame, grudge, menaces or displeasure, according to the old ancient order.

Finally, that the old privilege of the House be observed, which is that
15 they and theirs might be at liberty, frank and free, without arrest, molestation, trouble or other damage to their bodies, lands, goods or servants, with all other their liberties, during the time of the said parliament, whereby they may better attend and do their duty; all which privileges I desire may be enrolled, as at other times it hath been
20 accustomed.

Speech of Speaker Williams, 1562, in Sir Simonds D'Ewes, *Journals*, 1682, pp 65–6

2 (b) The Queen's Reply to a Petition for Privileges 1559

. . . To these petitions the Queen's Majesty hath commanded me (the Lord Keeper) to say unto you that her Highness is right well contented to grant them unto you as largely as amply and as liberally as ever they were granted by any of her noble progenitors; and to confirm the same with as
5 great authority. Marry, with these conditions and cautions; first, that your access be void of impunity, and for matters needful, and in time convenient. For the second, that your diligence and carefulness be such, Mr Speaker, that the defaults in that part be as rare as may be; whereof her

Majesty doubteth little. For the third, which is liberty of speech,
10 therewith her Highness is right well contented, but so as they be neither
unmindful or uncareful of their duties, reverence and obedience to their
sovereign. For the last, great heed would be taken that no evil disposed
person seek of purpose that privilege for the only defrauding of his
creditors and for the maintenance of injuries and wrongs. These
15 admonitions being well remembered, her Majesty thinketh all the said
liberties and privileges well granted . . . .

Sir Simonds D'Ewes, *Journals*, 1682, pp 16–17

Questions

a What evidence is there that the Commons were demanding 'ancient'
privileges (2(a) line 13)? How 'ancient' were they?

b Summarise the privileges demanded by the Commons.

* c If the queen was prepared to grant 'liberty of speech' (2(b) line 9),
why did this issue become an acute problem in her reign?

* d Comment on Strickland's case of 1571 and the arrest of Peter
Wentworth in 1576, 1587 and 1593 in the light of the Commons'
privilege of 'freedom from arrest'.

* e What developments in parliamentary privileges were there in
Elizabeth's reign?

3 The Queen's Marriage and the Succession 1566

(a) *August* 10, 1566: Parliament is to open at the beginning of October
and summonses have been sent to all those who usually attend. They say
that the Queen's only intention in calling it is to obtain large supplies, and
to defer the question of succession and her marriage . . . .

5 *September* 14, 1566: It is believed for certain that Parliament will
meet . . . . They think that if the Queen does not marry or proclaim a
successor, they will not vote her any supplies . . . .

October 19, 1566: . . . I have been informed that in the House of
Commons great difference existed yesterday as to whether the question
10 of the succession should be discussed before voting supplies, some said
that the succession was the prime cause of calling them together, and
should be one of the reasons for granting supplies; others that the
succession should not be discussed until supplies were voted, as they
thought it was disrespectful to seem to force the Queen in this way.

15 *October* 26, 1566: The discussion about the succession still goes
on . . . three days ago (the Queen) told me . . . that they had offered her
votes of £250,000 on condition that she would agree to (their
nomination), but she refused and said that she would not accept any
conditions, but that the money should be given freely and graciously, as it
20 was for the common good and advantage of the Kingdome and the
defence of Ireland . . . .

November 13, 1566: . . . the Queen seeing that they were determined to carry on the discussion about the succession, sent them an order telling them not to do so, but . . . the members thought that during the sittings
25 they had full liberty to treat upon matters beneficial to the country: they have greatly resented the order, and I am told that the Council have used their efforts with the Queen to allow Parliament to discuss freely this and other matters, since the confirmation of their acts rests with her.
December 2, 1566: . . . The grants have now been made but to a smaller
30 amount that was proposed. The Queen asked for £300,000 English money, in three instalments, and they have voted £200,000 in two . . . .
January 5, 1567: The Queen went to Parliament . . . and . . . dissolved it altogether; as I am told she is dissatisfied with the representatives of the people who form it . . . .

Letters of the Spanish Ambassador, Don D. G. de Silva, to Philip
II in *Calendar of State Papers, Spanish, 1558–1567*, i, pp 571–607

(b) *November* 9, 1566: Mr. Vice-Chamberlain declared the Queen's Majesty's express commandment to this House, that they should no further proceed in their suit, but to satisfy themselves with her Highness' promise of marriage (given 5th November) . . . .
5 *November* 11, 1566: Paul Wentworth, one of the burgesses, moved whether the Queen's commandment was not against the liberties . . . .
November 12, 1566: Mr. Speaker, being sent for to attend upon the Queen's Majesty at the court . . . at his coming (back) . . . began to show that he had received a special commandment from her Highness to
10 this House, notwithstanding her first commandment, that there should not be further talk of that matter . . . .
November 25, 1566: Mr. Speaker, coming from the Queen's Majesty, declared her Highness' pleasure to be that, for her good will to the House, she did revoke her two former commandments . . . which revocation
15 was taken . . . most joyfully . . . .

Commons' Journals, I, 76–7

Questions

a   Using 3(a) and 3(b), write an account of the parliamentary session of 1566–7 (of the second parliament of 1563–7). How (i) accurate (ii) reliable will this account be?
* b   Why did Elizabeth need 'large supplies' (3(a) line 3) by 1566 and why was this demand likely to be unpopular?
* c   Why was the question of marriage and succession such a serious one at this time? What attempts had been made to resolve it?
d   What do these extracts reveal about the way in which Elizabeth 'managed' the Commons?
* e   Who 'won' in this session: Crown or Parliament?

4 Freedom of Speech

(a) . . . Amongst other, Mr. Speaker, two things do great hurt in this place, of the which I do mean to speak. The one is a rumour which runneth about the House, and this it is, 'Take heed what you do, the Queen liketh not such a matter; whosoever prefereth it, she will be
5   offended with him': or the contrary, 'Her Majesty liketh of such a matter; whosoever speaketh against it, she will be much offended with him.' The other: sometimes a message is brought into the House, either of commanding or inhibiting, very injurious to the freedom of speech and consultation. I would to God, Mr. Speaker, that these two were buried in
10 hell, I mean rumours and messages . . . .

. . . Mr. Speaker, brought the last session (1572) into the House (a message) that we should not deal in any matters of religion but first to receive from the bishops. Surely this was a doleful message . . . . Truly I assure you, Mr. Speaker, there were divers of this House that said
15 that . . . God . . . was the last session shut out of doors. But what fell of it, forsooth? His great indignation was therefore poured upon this House, for he did put into the Queen's Majesty heart to refuse good and wholesome laws for her own preservation, the which caused many faithful hearts . . . grief . . . and moved all papists, traitors to God and
20 her Majesty . . . in their sleeves to laugh all the whole Parliament House to scorn . . . . So certain it is, Mr. Speaker, that none is without fault, no, not our noble Queen, since then her Majesty hath committed great fault, yea, dangerous faults to herself . . . .

Speech of Peter Wentworth, 8 February 1576, in Sir Simonds D'Ewes, *Journals*, pp 236–40

(b) . . . Her Majesty granteth you liberal but not licentious speech, liberty therefore but with due limitation. For even as there can be no good consultation where all freedom of advice is barred, so will there be no good conclusion where every man may speak what he listeth, without
5   fit observation of persons, matters, times, places and other needful circumstances. It shall be meet therefore that each man of you contain his speech within the bounds of loyalty and good discretion, being assured that as the contrary is punishable in all men, so most of all in them that take upon them to be counsellors and procurators of the commonwealth.
10 For liberty of speech, her Majesty commandeth me to tell you that to say yea or no to bills, God forbid that any man should be restrained or afraid to answer according to his best liking, with some short declaration of his reason therein, and therein to have a free voice, which is the very true liberty of the House; not, as some suppose, to speak there of all causes as
15 him listeth and to frame a form of religion or a state of government as to their idle brains shall seem meetest. She saith no King fit for his state will suffer such absurdities, and though she hopeth no man here longeth so much for his ruin as that he mindeth to make such a peril to his own safety, yet that you may better follow what she wisheth, she makes of her

20   goodness you the partakers of her intent and meaning . . . .
Speech of the Lord Keeper, 19 February 1593, printed by J. E.
Neale in Eng. Hist. Rev., XXXI (1916) pp 136–7

Questions

a   Why did Elizabeth resort to 'rumours and messages' (4(a) line 10)? In what other ways could she hope to influence Commons' discussions?

b   What evidence is there in 4(a) that Wentworth was interested in freedom of speech as a means to an end?

*   c   What were the consequences for Peter Wentworth of his 1576 speech?

d   Summarise and comment upon Elizabeth's concept of what constituted freedom of speech (4(b)).

5   Opposition in 1601: Monopolies

Mr Francis Bacon said: . . . I confess the bill [Mr. Laurence Hide's Bill '*An Act for the explanation of the Common Law in certain cases of Letters Patents*'] . . . is . . . ponderous and weighty . . . the use hath been ever by petition to humble ourselves unto her Majesty and by petition to
5 desire to have our grievances redressed, especially when the remedy toucheth her so nigh in prerogative . . . .

Mr Francis Moore: Mr Speaker, I know the Queen's prerogative is a thing curious to be dealt withal, yet all grievances are not comparable. I cannot utter with my tongue . . . the great grievances that the Town and
10 country, for which I serve, suffer by some of these monopolies. It bringeth the general profit into a private hand . . . . We have a law for the true and faithful currying of leather: there is a patent that sets all at liberty, notwithstanding that statute. And to what purpose is it to do anything by act of parliament, when the Queen will undo the same by her
15 prerogative? . . .

Sir Robert Wroth: . . . There have been divers patents granted since the last Parliament [1597]; these are now in being, viz. the patents for currants, iron, powder, cards, horns, ox· shin-bones, train—oil, transportation of leather, lists of cloth, ashes, bottles, glasses, bags, shreds of
20 gloves, aniseed, vinegar, sea-coals, steel, aqua—vitae, brushes, pots, salt, saltpetre, lead, accidences, oil, calamine stone, oil of blubber, fumathoes or dried pilchards in the smoke, and divers others.

    Upon the reading of the patents aforesaid, *Mr. Hakeweill of Lincoln's Inn* stood up and asked thus: Is not bread there? . . . if order be not taken
25 for these, bread will be there before the next Parliament . . . .

Mr Secretary Cecil: . . . This dispute draws two great things in question; first, the prince's power; secondly, the freedom of Englishmen . . . . And

you, Mr Speaker, should perform the charge her Majesty gave unto you
at the beginning of this parliament not to receive bills of this nature; for
30 her Majesty's ears be open to all grievances . . . .

Mr Speaker: It pleased her Majesty to command me to attend upon her
yesterday . . . from whom I am to deliver unto you all her Majesty's
most gracious message . . . . She said that . . . she understood that
divers patents which she had granted were grievous to her sub-
35 jects . . . but . . . she herself would take present order of reformation
thereof . . . . Some should be presently repealed, some suspended, and
none put in execution but such as should first have a trial according to the
law for the good of the people . . . .

H. Townshend, *Historical Collections*, 1680, pp 230–49

Questions

* *a* What was the *original* purpose of monopoly rights established by
      letters patent?
   b What grievances concerning monopolies are brought out in these
      extracts?
* *c* Why did monopolies become so important in the 1590s?
   d Comment on the view expressed by Mr Secretary Cecil.
* *e* 'Her master-stroke in parliamentary management' – what con-
      cessions did the queen make and why did she make them?

6   'Merely Potentiality'?

There has been no shortage of eloquent advocacy of the theory that
parliament, and especially the House of Commons, was set upon a new
career in the sixteenth century. For this theory we are mainly indebted to
specialists in Tudor history, principally to A. F. Pollard, G. R. Elton and
5   Sir John Neale . . . .
    What is basically important to Sir John is (1) to dispose of the legend of
Tudor despotism, (2) 'to banish the old illusion that early Stuart
parliaments had few roots in the sixteenth century,' and (3) to establish
that by the end of the century 'parliament had become a political force
10 with which the Crown and government had to reckon', this being 'a
change . . . brought about by developments in the power, position and
prestige of the House of Commons.' But Sir John's more particular task is
to elucidate these problems by discovering the 'vital significance' for the
growth of parliament, of the reign of Elizabeth I. Well aware of the
15 fewness of her parliaments and the brevity of their sessions . . . he makes
it abundantly clear that the age was still one of personal monarchy and
rightly insists that parliament was not an ordinary but an extraordinary
part of the constitution, and that it was none of its business to exercise
supervision over the government of the country. [Roskell concedes that

20 Sir John succeeds in his first and second basic aims] . . . But what of the
third? . . . .

Sir John has summarised developments in the position of the
Commons between Henry VIII's accession and Elizabeth I's: 'the House of
Commons had acquired the right, not the exclusive right, to control the
25 attendance of its members; it had created for itself the right to enforce the
privilege of freedom from arrest; it had invented a power to imprison
offenders against its dignity and privileges; it had converted an uncertain
prescriptive enjoyment of free speech into a formal privilege possessing
revolutionary possibilities . . . .' This is a fair statement. But . . . it is of
30 first rate importance to recognise a distinction between privileges which
affected the power of the Lower House over its own members . . . and
those which affected its power to control or influence the government.

Of all these privileges mentioned by Sir John the most important was
the privilege of free speech . . . . The Commons' right to speak and vote
35 against government measures, won by the time of Elizabeth's succession,
was something negative. What Elizabeth's reign produced, says Sir John,
was an opposition which 'wanted to initiate: to introduce bills and
motions of their own, to frame the agenda of parliament', and needed
freedom of speech in order to do so. But when we are considering the
40 *power* of the Commons in that period, surely what we must ask is, first,
whether the privilege upon which that desire depended for its realisation
was really enjoyed, and, second, whether that desire itself was actually
fulfilled.

What chiefly upset the relations between Elizabeth and the Commons
45 in the first half of her reign was the question of the royal succession and,
more especially, religious and ecclesiastical issues. And 'the conflicts and
divergences' between them were such that 'there was not a session free
from collision of some sort'. But there is no doubt that the Commons'
enlarged claim to freedom of speech was contested. What is more, it was
50 generally contested by the queen with success. Elizabeth, as Dr. Elton
says, 'put precisely those things out of bounds which the opposition
wished to discuss', and the defence of freedom of speech itself in 1576
by Peter Wentworth only resulted in his imprisonment in the
Tower . . . (and) .Wentworth's propensity to bold utterances again
55 resulted in his commital in 1587. Then, at the outset of the parliament in
1593, Elizabeth defined liberty of speech in terms which went far to
repudiate the Commons' claim . . . . Wentworth's third imprisonment . . . later in the same session, suitably enforced the queen's
warnings. What Wentworth's imprisonments for audacious speaking
60 surely indicate is that the right he claimed was largely illusory in
practice. . . . Although parliament, by Sir John's showing was less
tractable than used to be thought . . . that the queen was able to control
her Commons and curb their fantasies is surely a tribute less to the
growing power of the Lower House than the continuing power of the
65 sovereign. In controlling her Commons, Elizabeth sacrificed little if
anything, certainly nothing vital, of her prerogative. Restiveness in

opposition is not power, although it may lead to a claim to
it. . . . Elizabeth's policy towards parliament was co-operation – and
through members of her Privy Council in the Lower House she was in a
70   fair way to obtain it – but, if she failed to obtain it, then mastery. In Sir
John's considered judgement, 'from the constitutional point of view, the
most important theme in our story is the relationship of the Puritan
Movement to parliamentary development.' We may use his own words
as comment: that by 1601, 'there was no longer a Puritan organisation in
75   the background, and the fanatical mentality of bygone assemblies was in
disrepute.' So much for the threat to personal monarchy and preparation
of the constitutional revolution of Stuart times . . . . It would appear
that the real break in the history of the Commons comes not with the
Tudor period . . . It comes, rather, with the end of the power of the
80   Crown to govern effectively without parliament [in Roskell's view, at
the turn of the seventeenth century]. What the Tudor Commons had
been creating by organising their own self-discipline . . . was not power,
much less authority, merely potentiality.

J. S. Roskell, 'Perspectives in English Parliamentary History', in
Bulletin of the John Rylands Library, XLVl 1964, pp 455–74

Questions

* a   What is meant by 'the legend of Tudor despotism' (lines 6–7)?
* b   ' . . . the fewness of her parliaments and the brevity of their sessions'
(lines 14–15): how did Elizabeth's reign compare with the period
1485–1558?
c   What divergence of opinion between Sir John Neale (and others) and
J. S. Roskell is revealed in this extract?
d   What arguments does Roskell put forward to support his views?

7   Too Much Evidence?

It has become conventional to say that during the Elizabethan period
there was a great increase in the vigour and self-assertiveness of
Parliament. It has also become conventional to say that in Parliament the
Commons were gaining importance at the expense of the Lords. These
5   propositions appear to be true because we can read Commons'
speeches . . . because an increasing number of members were keeping
diaries of the proceedings of the Commons, and these diaries, unlike the
dry, formal minutes which make up the official *Journals*, give us the cut
and thrust of debate. By comparison we are in almost total ignorance of
10   the debates in the early Tudor Commons, and of the debates in the Lords
at any time in the century.
    It may well be, then, that the diaries have deceived us into thinking that
the Commons were becoming more important, and that a Lords' diary or
a Commons' diary of an early Tudor Parliament, would have given us a

15 very similar impression. We cannot say that the improvement of records
itself proves that the Commons were becoming more important, since
the bulk of records of all other types increased equally rapidly at the same
time. Since this increase in the bulk of records dominates our picture of
the period, it is unfortunate that we do not know why it happened. It may
20 have happened, as Francis Bacon suggested, because a sense of rapid
change strengthened the desire to make records, or it may have happened
for a reason so prosaic as a fall in the price of paper . . . .

    Conrad Russell, *The Crisis of Parliaments: English History 1509–
1660*, 1971, pp 218–9

Questions

a Which diarists have been quoted in this section? Who were they?

b Why might diaries have 'deceived us' (line 12) about the true position
of the Commons in Elizabeth's reign?

* *c* What are the merits and defects of diaries (or autobiographies) as
historical source material?

* *d* What are the advantages, and the disadvantages, of the *Commons'
Journals* in this period?

* *e* Can you suggest other reasons for the proliferation of record material
in Elizabeth's reign?

IX *English Foreign Policy*
1558—1603

Introduction

In 1558 England and Spain were allied against France, and the French king was supporting the claims of his daughter-in-law Mary, queen of Scots, to the English throne. Thirty years later England, supported by France and Scotland, was at war with Spain.

By 1570 Spain, England's ally for practically the whole of the previous eighty years, was becoming the arch-enemy. Religious differences and undeclared war 'beyond the line' had helped to shape the new situation, but it is not likely that these factors, by themselves, would have led to war.

The key to the changing European scene was the situation in the Spanish Netherlands which threatened England strategically and commercially. Traditional intense Anglo-Flemish commercial rivalry had led, as early as 1563—4, to mutual embargoes on trade, which was cut completely a decade later after the outbreak of the Dutch protestant revolt against Spanish overlordship. Increasingly the English government had to seek trade outlets in ports such as Holland and Zealand, which were under independent Dutch control. The actions of the government in 1568, 1572 and in 1585 showed just how far England was prepared to go to keep the Dutch revolt alive, even if this meant incurring Spanish wrath.

Elizabeth, anxious to delay the conflict that was implicit in the worsening relations between England and Spain — (there was increasing Spanish support for Roman Catholic missionaries in England; there were Spanish intrigues in Ireland; and Spain's ambassadors were implicated in plots against the queen) — was prepared, much to the exasperation of her ministers such as Walsingham, to negotiate not only with protestants in the Netherlands, in France and in Scotland, but also with Spain, Mary, queen of Scots, and catholic France.

As early as 1570 negotiations were taking place concerning the marriage of Elizabeth to a French prince. In 1572 England and France were allied by the treaty of Blois — the same year as the massacre of protestants on St Bartholomew's eve. France might be catholic but she was not as uncompromisingly catholic as Spain; the latter did not even have the equivalent of the Huguenots, and France was anti-Spanish even to the extent of supporting the protestant rebels in the Spanish Netherlands.

Open conflict between England and Spain began in 1585 and thereafter to 1604 a state of hostilities existed between the former allies. Two years before the Armada sailed the treaty of Berwick (1586) bound England and Scotland in a defensive alliance which the execution in 1587 of Mary, queen of Scots did nothing to disturb. In 1588 the accession of the Huguenot Henry IV (following the assassination of Henry III), sealed the Anglo–French accord, which not even Henry's conversion to catholicism in 1593 (*Paris vaut une messe*) could break; and the Anglo–French relationship lasted as long as the Spanish war.

Further Reading

P. S. Crowson, *Tudor Foreign Policy* (1973) part IIc, is a useful introduction for students. The most authoritative work on foreign policy is that by R. B. Wernham, especially *Before the Armada: the Growth of English foreign policy, 1485–1588* (1966); and his essays, 'English policy and the revolt of the Netherlands' in Bromley and Kossman (eds) *Britain and the Netherlands* (1960), (in which he argues that Elizabeth's policy in the Netherlands was inspired as much by fear of France as by fear of Spain), and 'Elizabethan War Aims and Strategy', in *Elizabethan Government and Society* (1961), quoted on pp 114–16, (in which he measures the discrepancy between Elizabeth's resources and her achievements). Wernham's defence of the queen against traditional criticism is not shared by C. H. Wilson, whose *Queen Elizabeth and the Revolt of the Netherlands* (1970) dismisses Elizabeth's policy as both frivolous and incompetent. See also Garrett Mattingly's *Renaissance Diplomacy* (1955), his *The Defeat of the Spanish Armada* (1959), and Pieter Geyl's *Revolt of the Netherlands* (2nd ed. 1958).

1   The Situation in 1560

Her Majesty now needeth not to have any kind of fear of the French King or the King of Spain for any damage they can do to her Highness any manner of ways. . . . As likewise, whereas Her Majesty oweth one million of ducats, I am right assured that King Philip and the French King 5   oweth each of them apiece 20 millions, so that all things considered, Her Majesty is in better case than the proudest prince of them all . . . . Here is a Scot come from Dieppe, who was there as (on) the 10th of this present, who saith that the French King hath no ships in a readiness and (he) lack(s) both money and men to put in them; and that now he hath more need to 10   have men about himself for to defend the great power that is up in France for to subdue M. de Guise and his brethren.

> Sir Francis Gresham, Antwerp, 16 June 1560, in K. de Lettenhove, *Relations politiques des Pays–Bas et de l'Angleterre 1555–1579*, 1882–1900, Vol II, p 463

Questions

* *a* What evidence, apart from that included in the extract, could be used to support Gresham's view that Elizabeth, in mid 1560, need have no fear of either France or Spain?
  b Identify 'the French King'.
  c Explain the reference to 'M. de Guise and his brethren' (line 11).
* *d* 'All things considered, Her Majesty is in better case than the proudest prince of them all.' Do you agree with this assessment?

2 The Treaty of Edinburgh 1560

. . . All military forces, as well by land as by sea, on both sides, shall withdraw from the Kingdom of Scotland.

. . . Except that so many French soldiers only may stay and remain in the castle of Dunbar and the fortress of Inchkeith as shall be agreed upon
5 between the French Orators and the Scottish nobility . . . .

Since the Kingdoms of England and Ireland lawfully belong and appertain to the said most Serene Lady and Prince Elizabeth . . . it is determined, agreed and contracted that the said Most Christian King and Queen Mary, and each of them, shall from henceforth abstain from using
10 or bearing the said title or arms of the Kingdom of England or Ireland . . . .

The said Most Christian King and Queen desire that this their benevolence towards their subjects be communicated to the aforesaid Most Serene Queen Elizabeth . . . through whose intercession and
15 request the said King and Queen have the more readily inclined their minds to this; therefore . . . it is contracted that the said Most Christian King and Queen Mary shall accomplish all which was granted by their said Orators to the nobility and people of Scotland at Edinburgh on 6 July in this present year 1560 . . . .

Rymer, *Foedera*, XV, p 594

Questions

* *a* How would you account for the timing of the treaty of Edinburgh?
  b What were the main terms of the Treaty?
  c Comment on the section (lines 6–11) relating to the lawful title to the English throne.
* *d* To extent did this treaty establish good relations between (i) England and France (ii) England and Scotland?

3 Anglo–Spanish Relations

(a) *Spanish Ships and Gold brought into Plymouth*

London, March 4, 1568

Twenty-two ships from Spain and Lisbon have recently come into the port of Plymouth here. Others are said to be on their way. These ships were brought in by force. They contain amongst other things spices and a Spanish mission. The latter has arrived in London. Every day the
5 Spaniards ask permission of the court to journey with the despatches to Flanders . . . .

For some time the Spanish Ambassador was escorted by a guard, but this has recently been dispensed with. The Beggars dislike this, for they would prefer that open war should break out between Spain and
10 England . . . .

The Spanish gold now here is said to come from Plymouth, ninety-five chests of it, as well as another fifty-four which ought to have gone to Antwerp. It amounts all in all to nearly £100,000. What the Queen will do with it time will reveal . . . . Such of this money as belongs to the
15 merchants Her Majesty is gracious enough to allow to be charged in Antwerp, but what belongs to the King of Spain . . . she thinks it right to withhold from the Duke of Alva.

(b) *Hawkins and Drake*

Seville, December 7, 1569

. . . John Hawkins recently passed Cape St. Vincent with twenty-five well found ships, among which are stated to be three of seven hundred tons, thirteen of three hundred, and the rest smaller . . . . Drake must now be close to the West Indian islands. At this juncture the ships from
5 New Spain would certainly be loaded up and on their way, so that the Englishman would have them at his mercy. Don Melendez is neither sufficiently armed, nor has he enough equipment and men to face Drake . . . . And the most annoying part of this affair is that this Hawkins could not have fitted out so numerous and so well equipped a
10 fleet without the aid and secret consent of the Queen. This conflicts with the agreement for the sake of which the King sent an Envoy Extraordinary to the Queen of England. It is the nature and habit of this nation not to keep faith, so the Queen pretends that all has been done without her knowledge and desire. The French write that their King
15 Francis (1) owing to the tricks played on him during his reign by the English, always had on his lips the following epigram:

'Anglicus, Anglicus est cui nunquam credere fas est,
Tum tibi dicit ave, tanquam ab hoste cave.'

. . . The real reason for this expedition and the further damage it will
20 cause we shall soon learn. May the Almighty protect us from still worse things!

The Fugger News Letters (2nd series), 1568–1605, pp 3, 7–8

Questions

* *a* How accurate is the account in 3 (a) of the seizure of the treasure ships?
  b Who were the 'Beggars' (3(a) line 8) and why did they want war between Spain and England?
* *c* Why did the queen want to withhold gold from the duke of Alva?
* *d* What did Hawkins and Drake contribute to the worsening of Anglo–Spanish relations?
  e What do these extracts reveal about the nature of Elizabeth's foreign policy at this time?

4 The Situation in the Netherlands 1572, as seen by an Englishman

Good Mr. Hoggyns . . . We also hear of a great league made with France which is thought that thereby the French pretendeth some further such to serve their turn: God of his goodness keep the noble isle of England to live without giving over much credit to foreign friendship. Here is great
5 preparation as ever I saw for within these twenty days there will be ten thousand horsemen and fifty thousand footmen: likewise be there 80 sail of men of war. Don John of Austria is come with his galleys to Genova and the Venetians goeth outwarde against the Turk who hath augmented their forces. The duke of Savoy armeth for the King 8000 footmen and as
10 it is said cometh himself in person. Flushing saluted the duke de Medina very vile at his coming and burned iii ships of merchants only by treason of a Flushing varlet that came out of Spain with them and took upon him to lead them into the port of Sluys and set them on ground himself went his way yet the day after the wind being very good the rest of the duke's
15 army hoisted up sail, and in despite of the town of Flushing passed to the Rannekens without hurt more than one gonner slain. The portyngall fleet of this country like false traitors struck anchor before Flushing which is like that many thereby are undone; The gensys [sic] took of the iii ships that were boarded XXXVI Spaniards and in the town hung them.
20 Likewise the Spaniards about XV days past took XXX French horsemen coming to Mons among which as it is said the son of Monsieur Montgomery was one who offered for his ransom 5000 crowns he and the rest of his companions were hanged at Flyford VI days past so that here is no favour but hanging on both sides. Our countrymen and
25 women as my lady of Northumberland lieth at Maklynge and so doth Mr. Daykeres [Dacres] where not many days past (two) of my L. Setones sons were like to have been slain in the tumult which standeth yet but in a mamerynge [sic] yet now they begin to come cooler and to obey the magistrates. The poor earl of Westmoreland lieth at Louvain and so doth
30 my lady Hungerford my old Knight and others . . . .

    Though I begone, write I pray you to me and send your letters to my L. to Bruges and in so doing I will write to you weekly from the camp of our occurrence. In haste written this present Tuesday the XVII of June at Bruges 1572.

Your loving friend
Thomas Parker.

To his loving friend Mr. Robert Hoggyns
at Mr. Edmunde Hoggyns his house in Milk Street
give this. At London.

Questions

* a What 'great league' (line 1) had recently been made between England and France? What were its main provisions?
* b What were the reasons which drove (i) England, and (ii) France to make this agreement?
* c What earlier agreements had been made with France between 1558 and 1572?
  d Suggest reasons why Mr Parker is obviously distrustful of a French alliance.
  e What information does the letter contain about French activity in the Netherlands and of her relationship with Spain?

5 A French Embassy

London, April 29, 1581.
Some distinguished representatives of France, many nobles and some legal experts are here. What they are after is not yet clearly proven. The French give out that they are negotiating the marriage of the Queen with the Duke of Alencon. Others declare that they are here to erect a firm
5 alliance between the French crown and the Low Countries to be under the direction of the Duke of Alencon. This would concern England too, as it could only be accomplished with the previous knowledge, good will and permission of the Queen. She has promised to lend the French £200,000 if they give her the town of Calais so that she may make use of
10 it in the Low Countries War. The French are also to swear to preserve this alliance between the Queen and the Low Countries.
  It is thought too that something could be arranged against the King of Spain to help Don Antonio . . . .
The Fugger News Letters (2nd series) 1568–1605, pp 55–6

Questions

  a Identify the duke of Alencon.
* b How serious were the marriage negotiations between Elizabeth and Alencon?
* c Why would Elizabeth be concerned about French involvement in the Low Countries War?
* d Who was Don Antonio? Was anything done to help him?

6 Letter of Reprisal to a Merchant 1585

. . . Whereas . . . one Robert Kitchyn of Bristol, merchant, hath made proof before me that certain of his goods monies and merchandise were of late . . . detained in the ports of Spain by the King's order and authority there, and that the loss and damage unto him by reason of the
5 said stay and seizure arising doth amount to the sum of £6,500; whereupon the said Robert Kitchyn hath ready equipped, furnished, and victualled to the seas one ship called the *Gift of God* of Bristol, of the burthen of ci. tons . . . lxxx mariners and men of war, being victualled for four months and furnished with xxiiii cast pieces and fowlers of
10 iron . . . .
Know ye therefore that I . . . Lord Charles Howard, Lord Admiral . . . by virtue of her Majesty's . . . letters patent to me directed, do licence and authorise the said Robert Kitchyn to send unto the seas the said ship . . . and therewith to set upon by force of arms and to
15 take . . . any of the ships of goods of the subjects of the King of Spain in an ample manner as if it were in time of war between her Majesty and the said King of Spain . . . .
Given in London in the High Court of the Admiralty . . . the Xth of July, 1585.
High Court of Admiralty, Exemplification, 23, in G. W. Prothero, *Select Statutes and other Constitutional Documents*, 1913, pp 465–7

Questions

* *a* When and why did King Philip of Spain order the seizure of English goods in Spanish ports?
* *b* Apart from letters of marque, what other response did Elizabeth's government make to this challenge?
* *c* 'Covert war' – comment on the validity of this assessment of Anglo-Spanish relations by 1585.

7 Assistance to the Netherlands 1585

1 That the Queen of England should send to the United Provinces an aid of . . . 5,000 footmen and one thousand horse, under the conduct of a Governor–General who should be a person of quality and rank, well affected to the true religion, and under good chiefs and captains; all of
5 whom should be paid by the Queen, so long as the war lasts.
2 . . . The United Provinces, individually and collectively, bind themselves, when, by God's grace and her Majesty's assistance, they shall be re-established in peace and repose, to repay all that her Majesty shall have disbursed, as well for the levy of the troops and their transportation,
10 as for their wages . . . .
3 For greater assurance of the repayment the town of Flushing, the

castle of Rannekens, in the isle of Walcheren, and the town of Brille, with two fortresses in Holland shall within one month of the confirmation of the Contract be placed in the hands of such governors as it shall please her Majesty to appoint, to be kept by garrisons of her troops until her Majesty shall be completely repaid . . . .

15

J. Dumont, *Corps universel diplomatique*, 1728, v, p 454

Questions

* a Why did Elizabeth agree to large-scale intervention in the Dutch wars in 1585?
* b The Dutch commissioners (in June 1585) offered Elizabeth the sovereignty of the Netherlands: why did Elizabeth decline?
  c Suggest reasons why the Dutch insisted on an English commander of 'quality and rank' (line 3).
  d Why is great emphasis placed on Dutch repayment of England's expenses?
* e What part did England play in the Netherlands, 1585—7?

8 Secret Negotiations 1586

. . . As to Brodenham's [a servant of Parma] being sent hither by you, we have also caused some of our Council to speak with him, who declared but there was on your part a great inclination to re-establish a peace between us and the Catholic King; to which end (as he says) your
5 Excellency offers to procure authority from the King to treat with us by means of fitting persons, so soon as he should know that we were inclined to lend an ear thereto. As to which we conceive that by our public declaration, the King, as well as your Excellency, may have learned what was then our mind, and is so still, and how important are the reasons
10 which have moved us to interfere in these affairs, not being urged either by ambitions, or any desire for the shedding of blood, but only to make safe our own State and to free our ancient neighbours from misery and from slavery. And to these two ends we have directed our actions, with the resolution to continue them, notwithstanding that by indirect means
15 rumours have been spread, chiefly in the Low Countries that we were inclined to a peace, giving no heed to the safety and liberty of these our neighbours, who have moved us by compassion for their miseries, and for other just and important causes to aid them and defend them from perpetual ruin and captivity.
20 And therefore in this very great wrong has been done to us. For such is our compassion for their miseries that in no manner will we allow their safety to be separated from our own, knowing how the two depend on each other. And so we pray your Excellency to understand that this is our determination, notwithstanding any sort of rumours falsely spread
25 abroad to the contrary, greatly to our dishonour. Nevertheless, you may

be persuaded that if any reasonable conditions of peace should be offered
to us which tend to the establishing of our safety and honour and the
liberty of our neighbours, we shall no less willingly accept them than
unwillingly we have been forced to the contrary, seeing that in no way
30 can we do anything more pleasing to God Almighty than by embracing
the peace and safety of Christendom of which in these times, we who are
Princes and Monarchs have chiefly to think. And it is known to the
Omnipotent (the God of peace and Searcher of all human hearts) that to
this our heart has always been inclined, to whose judgement we appeal
35 against the malice of those tongues which strive to persuade the world to
the contrary.

> Elizabeth I to Alexander Farnese, Duke of Parma, 8 July 1586, in
> *Letters of Queen Elizabeth I*, ed. Harrison

Questions

a Who was the duke of Parma?
b Comment on Elizabeth's declared reasons for involvement in the
   Low Countries – 'these two ends' (lines 11–13, 21–3).
c What 'rumours' about Elizabeth's intentions had been spread?
   Comment on her reference to 'indirect means' (line 14).
d What was the *real* value of these negotiations from Elizabeth's point
   of view?

9 The Armada: the Marquis de Santa Cruz Urges Delay 1587

Sire,

. . . If it be really decided to go to England itself I would only observe
that this Armada, even when united with the troops of the Duke of
Parma, which would at this season be embarked and carried over the
straits with no small difficulty, does not seem to me sufficient to attempt
5 this enterprise in the very heart of the winter. We have no harbours at
hand in case of need, and the tide is extremely strong, the sea all open to
the south winds. Nor, in my opinion, would it be such an easy matter to
take the Isle of Wight, or any other harbour, for the shelter of our
fleet . . . .
10   . . . . It is my opinion that the sailing of the Armada should be delayed,
if not till March [1587], at least till the middle of February, to allow the
weather to grow milder. And your majesty must remember that should
any misfortune befall the fleet, which God forbid, it would be impossible
to put together another such Armada for a long time to come. To me it
15 seems that a sovereign with such a reputation in the world would not
allow himself to be swept away by a thirst for vengeance. . . . Should
your Majesty resolve to accept my advice I would still recommend that
the rumour should be circulated that the fleet is to sail at once, with a view

to frightening the Queen into an open course of action and compelling
20 her to instruct her agents to deal in earnest with the question of the total
restoration of Holland and Zealand . . . .

Calendar of State Papers, Venetian, 1581–1591, viii, pp 320–2

Questions

a What can be deduced from this letter about the Spanish plan of
invasion?
* b Was the sailing of the Armada delayed?
* c Why might the king of Spain's 'thirst for vengeance' (line 16) have
been increased in 1587?
d Explain the reference to 'Holland and Zealand' (line 21).

10 A Speech of Queen Elizabeth 1593

. . . It may be thought simplicity in me, that, all this time of my reign, I
have not sought to advance my territories, and enlarge my dominions;
for opportunity hath served me to do it. I acknowledge my womanhood
and weakness in that respect; but though it hath not been hard to obtain,
5 yet I doubted how to keep the things so obtained; and I must say, my
mind was never to invade my neighbours, or to usurp over any . . . .
Yet the King of Spain doth challenge me to be the quarreller, and the
beginner of all these wars: in which he doth me the greatest wrong that
can be, for my conscience doth not accuse my thoughts, wherein I have
10 done him the least injury: but I am persuaded in my conscience, if he
knew what I know, he himself would be sorry for the wrong that he hath
done me.
I fear not all his threatenings; his great preparations and mighty forces
do not stir me; for though he come against me with a greater power than
15 ever was his invincible navy, I doubt not . . . but that I shall be able to
defeat and overthrow him. I have great advantage . . . for my cause is
just . . . .
The subsidies you give me, I accept thankfully; if you give me your
good wills with them; but if the necessity of the times and your
20 preservations did not require it, I would refuse them; but . . . it is needful
for a princess to have so much always lying in her coffers for your defence
in time of need . . . .

Somer's Tracts, Vol I, p 463

Questions

* a What was the occasion of this speech in 1593?
b Comment on Elizabeth's explanation of her lack of an aggressive
foreign policy (lines 1–6).
* c How might the king of Spain support his contention that Elizabeth

had been 'the quarreller and the beginner of all these wars' (lines 7–
8)?

d   How accurate was Elizabeth's statement that she had not done the
    king of Spain 'the least injury' (line 10)?
e   Explain the reference to 'great preparations and mighty forces' (line
    13).

11   Elizabethan War Aims

*If the late Queen would have believed her men of war as she did her scribes, we
had in her time beaten that great empire in pieces and made their kings kings of
figs and oranges as in old times. But her Majesty did all by halves and by petty
invasions taught the Spaniard how to defend himself, and to see his own weakness*
5   *which till our attempts taught him, was hardly known to himself.* So did Sir
Walter Raleigh, looking back from James I's reign, reflect upon
Elizabeth's conduct of her war against Spain . . . . That verdict contains
both an assumption about Elizabeth's war aims and a criticism of her
methods. Let us begin by examining the assumption, for until we are sure
10 about the Queen's aims we cannot safely criticise her methods . . . . It
was never her aim to destroy Spain and 'break that great empire in pieces'.
England, she believed, needed a powerful Spain to countervail the power
of France. For Elizabeth, and the older generation of her scribes, had
grown up in a Europe dominated by the French monarchy and the House
15 of Hapsburg. . . . For at least the first decade of Elizabeth's reign, France
remained the enemy most to be feared, while it was Spanish power and
Spanish goodwill (or Spanish self-interest) that restrained the Pope from
excommunicating Elizabeth and deterred the French from executing his
unspoken censures.
20   However within a month of Mary [Stuart's] enforced abdication, the
duke of Alva marched into Brussels (August 1567) with a Spanish
army . . . . This was a move in Spanish domestic . . . rather than . . .
foreign policy; an expression of Philip II's purpose to be absolute
and Catholic master in all the many mansions that were his share of the
25 vast and rambling Hapsburg house. . . . Elizabeth . . . could no more
allow those countries [Netherlands territories] to be turned into the main
base of Spanish military power than she had been able to let Scotland
become a French citadel . . . .
        Yet this alarm from Spain did not end anxiety about France.
30 For . . . the Netherlands rebels were only too ready to call in the French
to save them from the Spaniards. And French armies, extending French
control of the coast from Calais to Flushing . . . would be even more
dangerous there than Spanish armies. As Sussex put it: 'the case will be
hard with the Queen and with England if ever the French possess or the
35 Spaniards tyrannise in the Low Countries.'
        Elizabeth's answer . . . was to try to persuade or force Philip II to recall
his armies and restore the Netherlands to their status under his father

Charles v, with some more tolerable settlement of their religious differences. Her pressure took many forms – diplomatic expostulation, the seizure of Alva's pay ships (1568), unofficial aid to the rebels, raids by Drake and his fellows upon Spanish America, a defensive alliance with France (1572). . . . The forms varied, but the purpose never changed and it was this that eventually brought England and Spain to war. There were, of course, other causes of quarrel. Disputes over English merchants' privileges in their great Netherlands markets; Philip's determination not to let Hawkins and his associates trade to Spanish America; the activities of the Inquisition in Spanish ports and of English privateers and pirates on the high seas; the difference of religion, which among other things made English ambassadors intolerable in Spain and turned Spanish ambassadors into Catholic plotters in England: all these played some part. Yet they could hardly themselves have brought the two governments to war . . . . It was Elizabeth's determination to frustrate Philip's policy in his Netherlands provinces that eventually brought him to the enterprise of England.

Even so, as long as France seemed capable of independent action and the Netherlands of prolonged resistance, Philip felt compelled to avoid a war with England and to yield somewhat to English pressure. . . . As things fell out, the growing divisions in the United Netherlands from 1578 onwards opened the way for Parma to reconquer the southern and eastern provinces. By the summer of 1585 with William the Silent assassinated (1584) and Antwerp fallen, the Spanish army looked within striking distance of final victory over the rebels. Just then Philip II was also able to eliminate all danger of French intervention. Anjou's death and the childlessness of Henry III left the Huguenot Henry of Navarre heir presumptive to the French throne. This drove the Catholic League and the Guises to take arms and place their cause under the protection of Spain. Their victory would make France the client of Spain. It would unite Catholic Europe under Spanish leadership . . . .

. . . Elizabeth could not allow Spain to destroy England's old enemy France. Yet, equally, she could not afford to destroy her new enemy, Spain. For England could live . . . in a world of two Leviathans; she could not live where there was but one . . . . A restored France, that was not matched by a powerful Spain would be, if possible, a worse danger to England than a triumphant Spain that was not matched by a strong France. For the same reasons, England must defend Dutch liberties, but would not fight for their independence. An independent Netherlands would be too weak to withstand a restored France and, if they became French, that would give France too dangerous a preponderance. So, while the whole Netherlands must be freed from Spanish armies . . . they must remain under the nominal sovereignty of the King of Spain, who alone had the power to defend them against their mighty neighbour.

The Queen had, of course, other war aims too . . . (but) there seems no real doubt that her principal war aim, the principal cause of the conflict

85 with Spain, was her determination to restore all the Netherlands
provinces to their ancient liberties and privileges . . . and to secure the
Netherlands Protestants 'their liberty of their profession and exercise of
the Christian religion'. But nominally Spanish they must remain. To this
policy she clung with extraordinary tenacity . . . .
90   She was not one of England's great war leaders and she only half
achieved her aims. Yet to have helped the French monarchy to its feet, to
have saved half the Netherlands from Spanish 'tyranny', to have kept the
other half out of French possession, and England itself out of bankruptcy,
was a fair achievement against the Spain of Philip II.

R. B. Wernham, 'Elizabethan War Aims and Strategy', in
*Elizabethan Government and Society, Essays presented to Sir J. E.
Neale*, ed. S. T. Bindoff *et al*, 1961 pp 340–6, 368

Questions

a   Comment on Wernham's assessment of the situation during 'the first
decade of Elizabeth's reign' (line 15).

b   Why was Elizabeth so concerned about the Netherlands and what
policy did she follow there?

c   Why did England and Spain go to war in 1585 – and not before?

* d   'Her Majesty did all by halves' (line 3); 'She only half achieved her
aims' (lines 90–91). Do you agree?